The Struggle for the Film

The Struggle for the Film
Towards a socially responsible cinema

HANS RICHTER

edited by Jürgen Römhild
translated by Ben Brewster
foreword by A. L. Rees

WILDWOOD HOUSE

Originally published in 1976 as
Der Kampf um den Film
Copyright © Carl Hanser Verlag München Wien, 1976

English edition first published in 1986 by
Scolar Press (cloth)
Wildwood House Ltd (paper)
Gower Publishing Company Ltd
Gower House, Croft Road, Aldershot
Hants, GU11 3HR, England

British Library Cataloguing in Publication Data
Richter, Hans
  The struggle for the film: towards a
  socially responsible cinema.
  1. Experimental films—History and
  criticism   2. Moving-pictures—Europe—
  History
  I. Title   II. Römhild, Jürgen   III. Der
  Kampf um den Film.   *English*
  791.43′094   PN1995.9.E96

  ISBN 0-7045-0552-5

Illustrations for Hans Richter and Man
Ray © ADAGP 1986, and for Fernand Léger
© DACS 1986

Printed in Great Britain at the
University Press, Cambridge

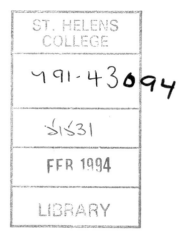

Contents

Foreword

by A. L. Rees

Hans Richter was a film-maker and an ardent supporter of the 'new cinema' which developed in Europe between the two world wars. This movement, which had wide social and aesthetic significance in its own time, celebrated the camera-eye, the film spectacle and the cubistic reordering of time and space through montage. It was hostile to the commercial industry, for here blatant business interests fought over the profit to be made from mass dreams and fantasies, and kept the cinema within firm conventions.

Written in the later 1930s and revised by the author for publication in 1976, *The Struggle for the Film* is about the situation of the new cinema in the highly politicised and anxious years that preceded the Second World War, by which time the avant-garde had adopted a social rather than aesthetic perspective. The first avant-garde cinema had emerged in the 1916–25 period, from the ferment of modern art; Cubism, Expressionism, Dada and Futurism. In Germany the movement was devoted to the abstract or 'absolute' film (with Oskar Fischinger, Walter Ruttmann, Viking Eggeling and Richter himself), while in France there developed a more figurative and lyricist avant-garde at the fringes of the industry (and sometimes – as with Gance, L'Herbier and Epstein – at its centre) which grew parallel to film-making by artists like Man Ray and Fernand Léger.[1]

The dynamism of the early period is reflected in the present book, which uses many examples taken from 20s film-making and continues to attack the grip of bourgeois, literary ideas on cinema at the expense of new forms of 'plastic expression' which exploit the unique properties of the medium itself. But *The Struggle* . . . was written in political exile, was not published, and – in 1939 – faced a postponement of the agenda for which it vigorously argued: the struggle for social cinema.

Richter had been closely involved with the film avant-garde for over twenty years when he wrote this polemical text. Born in 1888, he was an enthusiast of radical art from his student years, first as an Expressionist painter. Invalided to Switzerland in 1917 as a result of war injuries, he stayed on and joined the Dada group formed the year before at the Cabaret Voltaire. After the war he returned to Germany, where he was an active campaigner and publicist for 'Dada-constructivism', publishing in De Stijl, MA and G, which he edited from 1923–6. From his collaboration with the Swedish pioneer of abstract film, Viking Eggeling, came the 'Rhythm' films which occupied him until the mid-20s. He also worked in fashion and graphic design, and made commercials and special-effects inserts for feature films. Abandoning pure abstraction in 1926 with the elliptical montage of *Film Study*, his later personal films, including the comic 'trick-film' *Ghosts Before Breakfast* (1928), continued this vein of surreal fantasy.

Writing in 1946[2] from the United States, Richter discussed the pressure of social and political events on the avant-garde, as well as the advent of sound, which closed the international market for silent experimental 'shorts' and made production too expensive for most independent film-makers. The avant-garde consequently moved to those parts of the industry that offered employment, such as animation (as with Len Lye, Fischinger and Ruttmann). Film-makers also took up documentary production, which relied less on the profit motive than on state or public patronage, had social aspirations, allowed some technical experiment, and did not use actors. These distinguished the 'factual film' from the fictional, although the industry nonetheless adopted avant-garde techniques to extend the narrative language of the feature movie.

In 1929, the Stuttgart 'Film und Foto' exhibition published Richter's *Filmgegner von heute – Filmfreunde von morgen*[3] (Enemies of film today, friends of film tomorrow), to accompany the cinema section. With a witty photo-text of captions and frame–stills, the book demonstrates camera movements, editing, lenses, printing and montage, and challenges the kitsch and dramatics of commercial cinema. Those alienated from the cinema ('film's enemies today') can only be reclaimed as 'film's friends tomorrow' by creative and intelligent programming in the film societies. Film clubs at this time provided the only non-commercial public forum for film culture, and they were able to present advanced and un-censored work (*Battleship Potemkin*, for example, largely relied for its European distribution on the societies, of which there were famous examples in London, Paris and Berlin). They were thus a strong part of the 'cultural struggle', and Richter's book is effectively their manifesto.

Filmgegner ... also argues for a cinema aesthetic built on montage. By developing itself through the extension of its formal codes, film remains true to its own technology and becomes more productive. Richter suggests that such an independent cinema could successfully counteract commercial interests, and would find support from mass audiences. Although the book is still 'formalist' – it stresses the montage rather than the socialist content of Soviet films – these thoughts on form, production and exhibition are pre-cursors of the analysis in the later text presented here.

The Stuttgart show encouraged much international contact in 1929, especially between the Soviets and the Germans. Lissitsky, Tretyakov and Eisenstein came to Germany, and the Meyerhold troupe presented *Roar, China!* and *The Government Inspector* in Berlin. Brecht, whose contact with Richter dates from the 1920s, had earlier shaped his ideas in contact with Piscator and Russian ex-futurists like Tretyakov, for whom the destruction of illusionis-tic theatre ('laying bare the device') was itself a frontal attack on the bourgeoisie. Eisenstein regarded Meyerhold as his master. Connections were in the making, though with little time to flourish.

In September 1929, the first Avant Garde Film[4] conference was held at La Sarraz, Zurich – among those present were Richter, Ruttmann, Balázs, Moussinac, Montagu and Eisenstein. The con-gress topic shows the general turn of events: 'The art of cinema, its social and aesthetic purposes'. The second, and final, meeting in Brussels in 1930 went further, recognising that 'the Avant Garde as a purely aesthetic movement had passed its climax and was on the way to concentrating on the social and political film, mainly in documentary form.'[5] The first movement 'expired', in Richter's phrase, because political tensions 'made poetry no longer suitable', and artists decided to adopt a more practical commitment to

9

social action. 'Our age demands the documented fact' (p. 42).

In its predominantly aesthetic concerns, Richter's 1929 book to a degree lags behind his changing position, at a time when the energies that had gone into formal experiment were being channelled, under the 'social imperative', into documentary cinema. Left cultural policies in Germany centred on the Communist Party (KPD) and its supporters, among whom Richter was counted. He was living with the leading Communist actress Margarete Melzer, headed a 'progressive' group of film societies (the League for Independent Film), and in 1931 was assigned an anti-Nazi film, *Metall.* His fellow scriptwriter on this German–Soviet co-production was Pera Attasheva, Eisenstein's future wife, and the film was funded by the Prometheus distribution company, an offshoot of the Comintern cultural and publishing agency, AIH.[6]

Richter was shooting in the USSR when the Nazis came to power. *Metall,* which had already run into political problems, was abandoned. Richter spent the next years in exile, working in France and Switzerland. Towards the end of the decade he began to write *The Struggle for the Film.* Despite the setbacks in Europe, and the dispersal of the avant-garde, the documentary movement was strong. Following the defeat in Germany, the Soviets developed a new policy, the Popular Front against Fascism, a broad-based alliance which, as 'socialist realism' also flourished, did not encourage experiment in art. In his book Richter tries to deal with the conflicts and possibilities raised in this new period of struggle.

Compared to *Filmgegner . . .,* the present text shows the increased politicisation of the avant-garde and its move away from a 'formal' aesthetic. Almost uniquely among leftist cinéastes, however, Richter accepts neither socialist realism nor a documentary aesthetic. He explicitly rejects Rotha's notion of 'propagandist' socialist cinema. Propaganda derives from advertising, in which 'the consumers must be "coproduced" with the commodity' (p. 142) (Richter had worked on many commercials). He proposes instead a 'social dramaturgy' in which meaning is produced from a course of events shown in their context and process. Here he might have agreed with Walter Benjamin's definition of Brecht's Epic Theatre, recalled in Richter's formulation, which 'does not reproduce conditions, rather it discloses, it uncovers them.'

Part of the continuing value of *The Struggle for the Film* is that it escapes two main responses to domination of cinema by Hollywood and finance capital; the 'unmediated' documentary, and the model of a national 'art' cinema. It does so by the breadth of its references to film, and through two Brechtian precepts – that use-value in art is more important than aesthetic value, and that reality is transformed by the cinema's means of representation. A relatively isolated text when it was written, with theses which link it back to pre-Nazi Germany, it remains an important reflection of the Brecht group's response to the political crises and doctrinal disputes within the Comintern.

A prolific and influential historian of the avant-garde in which he participated, Richter's recollections cannot always be trusted. Strong challenges have been made to his account of the early experimental cinema, while his custodianship of Eggeling's works and reputation has been examined and severely criticised.[7] On rather different grounds, his 1964 book *Dada – Art and Anti-Art* contrasts with most recent studies of the movement by downplaying its political aspects (ironically, in the present context). In general, Richter was inclined to exaggerate his role, considerable though it was, in the history of the avant-garde.

The Struggle for the Film is a polemical and 'tendentious' book of a social and not a personal character. The question of 'authenticity' does not arise, except in a form which adds to the interest of the text. Richter writes not with hindsight but from within the struggle itself (on the assumption, as the editor states, that the late revision of the book does not affect its overall tone and temper). The questions and conflicts of cinema in the late 1930s described in the book are those faced by Richter as a film-maker. He is here in the thick of things. But the self-embedded politique of the book allows it to echo several voices apart from the author's, as Richter seems to formulate and extend further into the cinema the ideas of the 'modernist' marxists of the informal, international Brecht circle. For such a text to be mixed or multi-voiced is appropriate, and does not reflect adversely upon the skill of the author, for this group had long attacked individualism in art.

The book is in two parts, the first dealing with the history and contemporary role of the cinema. In terms of film's usage rather than its aesthetics, Richter outlines three kinds of development; documentary, fantastic and fiction film. Documentary is rooted in the earliest 'primal cinema', but has moved from the simple fascination with movement which satisfied the Lumières' audiences to a deeper concern for the events depicted. It has thus overcome, through the 'interpretative montage' of Flaherty, Ivens and Vertov, a former tendency to false aestheticism and pictorialist banality. Fantasy (or grotesque) film also originates from early cinema, which began in the fairground. Richter traces it through Méliès and the trick-film to Sennett's mad chases and Chaplin's slapstick, as well as to a more self-conscious form in the *Caligari* tradition. Fiction film arises from commercial antipathy to primitive film, and the consequent *embourgeoisement* of film form, drama and 'picture palaces' in the attempt to be both socially and financially successful. Nonetheless, this cinema has produced new techniques and language, including montage.

Richter now points to contradictions in the 1930s cinema. Avidly supported by the lower classes, films are aimed at the middle classes. The cinema does not address working-class problems, but only offers dreams to substitute for them. Richter demands a socially informed cinema to increase both the mass audience's knowledge of reality and its capacity to take part in changing it. Under capitalism, the cinema is a safety-valve for working-class aspirations. It is controlled by external censorship and internal conventions, which lead to smooth, unproblematic representation, 'universal' themes, subjectivist acting, and psychologistic reduction of plot and action.

The second part of the book turns to the 'progressive' cinema, which Richter finds scattered in a remarkable number of places. It includes: the visual acting style in Dreyer's *Joan of Arc*; surrealist multiplicity in Dulac; film lyricism in Delluc; the evocation of reality within conventional melodramas, as in *Cavalcade* and *Wedding March*; the denial of the individual hero in *Potemkin* and *La Grande Illusion*; the populist comedy of Chaplin and the Marx Brothers; Chaplinesque diversion from the linear narrative; the *cinéma-vérité* of Ivens; and the substitution of cinematic, 'musical' speech for the timing and manner of conventional stage speech, as in Guitry and Clair.

Richter also requests of a social, progressive cinema that it include the invisible world of the imagination in the reality which it depicts. Montage can unite 'the functional and the irrational', to show 'the intangible, the inconceivable, the enigmatic music of things, . . . as valuable as our pleasure in the knowledge of things' (p. 162). Richter's concept of a social cinema is clearly, defensibly, experimental.

The Struggle... develops the political analysis of cinema begun by Richter in the late-Weimar period, and its formulations are shared by Brecht, Tretyakov, Eisenstein and Benjamin (the first three of whom it acknowledges and quotes). In part, the book synthesises and extends the thought of a distinct if irregular axis of writers and artists, among the other stronger groups in the Popular Front.

Brecht is directly invoked by Richter on 'culinary' acting (p. 146), anti-psychologism and the need for 'cinematic gesture' appropriate to the audience's dissecting eye. Equally familiar is Richter's notion of interruption to the seamless narrative, the 'double' response of the spectator to illusionism and realism in art, and constructing opposition to 'naturalistic theatricality' around the aesthetic device (pp. 136–9). But not all brechtianisms come from Brecht – the theory that all objects are 'raw material' for the camera to transform has a history in avant-garde film going back to Jean Epstein.[8]

Richter's enthusiasm for the entertainment-value of films is, however, openly inflected by Brecht's 'pleasure of learning', in which, Richter says, laughter becomes 'the gateway to philosophy'. The pleasure principle allows Richter to include Chaplin, Dadaism and the fantastic film in the line he traces from the 'primal' film to the cinema of social struggle, just as realism can include popular fantasy, Soviet montage and the avant-garde. Here he parallels Brecht's notion that realism must be open enough to include the formal experiments which keep art in line with changing historical realities.

Benjamin is not directly cited by Richter, although *The Struggle*

. . . to a degree overlaps with Benjamin's more 'tendentious' essays, 'The author as producer' (1934) and 'The work of art in the age of mechanical reproduction' (1936).[9] The first refers to Tretyakov's interventionist journalism and Brecht's account of the intelligentsia, and describes montage (linked to Dada) as 'an interruption of the context in which it is inserted', a phrase which crosses Brecht's and Richter's use of 'interpolation'. In the 1936 essay, where film is seen as collective, 'authorless' production, examples are used which suggest a Brechtian reading of cinema, conditioned and informed by the experimental-formal film represented by Richter. The essay notes the transforming role of the camera, refers to Vertov, Dreyer and Pudovkin, condemns the industry, discusses film technology, argues that film can link artistic and scientific photography and asserts the unique analysis of gesture by film. 'By its transforming function', concludes Benjamin, 'the camera introduces us to unconscious optics as does psychoanalysis to unconscious impulses.'[10]

Despite their common ground, Benjamin remains more sceptical than Richter that the film audience can be active and participatory, on the model of epic theatre, and he stresses the passive, 'absent-minded' stare of the spectator in the cinema. The viewer is subjected to a series of 'shocks' characteristic of film, limiting the degree to which the audience can attain 'apperception', the state of analytical self-consciousness to which, Benjamin argues, the human subject is led by both Freud and the cinema. This scepticism seems shared by Brecht. In a diary entry of 1942 which notes his 'fundamental reproach' to cinema, Brecht notes the separation of production and consumption, the division between the 'fixed' film-performance and the viewers, 'the result of a production that took place in their absence.'[11]

While the unexpected citation of Valéry (p. 154) might have Benjamin as source, and possibly too some of the surrealist content of Part 2, the Freudian aspects of the book arguably share more with Eisenstein's amalgam of Pavlov and psychoanalysis.[12] Cinema is 'wish-fulfilment' (p. 104), and Richter calls 'abreaction' the cinema's ability to release nervous tension, which is ultimately social: 'one lives on a powder keg, and in the cinema one wants to

14

see it blow up at last' (p. 90). A content-analysis of a supposedly pacifist film shows that it really naturalises violence; here, the manifest-latent distinction is used as practical criticism (p. 107). Similarly, and like Brecht, Richter often refers to the process of 'working through', which might apply to a dream, a text or a social issue.[13] The key conjunctions here usually link Freud to a marxist analysis of art.

The pervasive influence of Eisenstein, as well as Benjamin, may be indicated in the references to the camera's 'fascination with allegories' and symbolism, as well as in many allusions to the role of montage. Richter tries 'to discover the language of an exclusively pictorial formula for an inner experience, a thought, an idea.' Images produce concepts, and here Richter quotes Eisenstein's statement that the 'visibility' of film, which can show abstractions through images, can abolish and overcome 'the antagonism between thought and feeling' (p. 163).

In the context of the Popular Front, Richter's book is oppositional, or at least deviant, in its defence of experiment, fantasy, the primacy of technological devices, and the extension of 'realism' to encompass montage and fragmentation. While Richter was working on it, Brecht (also exiled, in Denmark) was drafting his similarly unpublished response to Lukács and social realism, and he too defines 'realism' generously: 'For time flows on ..., methods become exhausted, stimuli no longer work. New problems appear and demand new methods. Reality changes; in order to represent it, modes of representation must also change. Nothing comes from nothing; the new comes from the old, but that is why it is new.'[14]

Displaced persons, the exiles take their bearings from 'over there', Brecht's phrase for Moscow, where Lukács and Eisenstein lived and where the fate of their friend Tretyakov was still unknown when Brecht and Benjamin discussed his arrest in the summer of 1938.[15] Returning to Paris from his visit to Brecht, Benjamin received the opening letter in his exchange with Adorno (editing the text from New York) about his 'Baudelaire' essay.[16] This dispute was itself overcast by Adorno's disapproval of Brecht, who he felt influenced Benjamin towards directly politicised and 'unmediated' connections between culture and economy.

Their dispute parallels the argument of Brecht against Lukács, just as both inflect a reading of Richter's account of the struggle for film. They share the same problematic, the social conditions of modern art and politics. The key figures from the past in these disputes – the Russian formalists for Brecht, Baudelaire for Benjamin – also prompt an extension of the questions at stake to the Soviet film-makers Vertov and Eisenstein who, in different conditions, were also attacked for intellectualist formalism. The western debate hinges on Adorno's and Benjamin's different views on how avant-garde art and commercial art are related under capitalism; 'the one subjectively progressive and objectively elitist, the other objectively popular and subjectively regressive'.[17] Almost alone in this period, Brecht aimed to be both advanced and popular, and this too represents Richter's ambition in *The Struggle.* . . .

Richter left Europe for the US in 1941, and continued to teach, make films and write. He arrived as a new avant-garde was forming among film-makers (it included Kenneth Anger, Maya Deren and Sidney Peterson), but Richter's later work was largely independent of it.[18] Although Brecht too was in the US from 1941–7, no new collaboration resulted and Brecht's Hollywood career took a different turn.

The historical interest of Richter's book (which he attempted to publish in America, without success) is in its attempt to understand the cinema politically and aesthetically, using the authority of 'Brechtian' thought, within an essentially polemical context. Unusually for the later 1930s, it neither rejects the radical aspirations of the avant-garde, nor adopts the prevailing 'populist' versions of socialist cinema. It stresses social function over art, but maintains that reality and content in film are constructed by the cinema, historically and technically. In rejecting a national 'art' cinema, it concentrates on the mass audience and the possibilities of cinema as struggle, within contradiction. Richter examines the social role of cinema, and how its reception by spectators can be changed, but remains interested in finding conflict and 'devices' already embedded in cinema. The struggle is already there in the cinema; it does not have to be imported.

An emphasis on entertainment as well as instruction is still rare in discussions of oppositional – and especially 'Brechtian' – film-making. In this book Richter maintains his links with the dynamism of the earlier avant-garde by his defence of humour in the cinema. His equal stress on montage in the construction of film meaning and form connect the book not only to the 1920s but also to later, and continuing, debates about the language of cinema, as does his early attempt to draw together formal, institutional and psycho-analytic aspects of film.

The Struggle . . . indicates, in an area still unexplored in detail, the politicisation of the film avant-gardes of the 1920s, and their response to social crisis in the 1930s. Its publication will help to illuminate a set of complex relationships in this crucial period of cultural and social history. It offers a fascinating view of these issues by a leading avant-garde film-maker allied to one of the most important radical groupings of the period, written with a direct aim; to accomplish the elusive union of art and politics in the cinema.[19]

NOTES

1. See Hans Richter, 'A History of the Avant-garde', in *Art in Cinema*, ed. F. Stauffacher, San Francisco, 1946. For more recent accounts see M. Le Grice, 'German Abstract Film in the Twenties', and Ian Christie, 'French Avant-garde Film in the Twenties', in *Film as Film*, Arts Council catalogue, 1979. A concise account of the movement is provided in David Curtis, *Experimental Cinema*, Studio Vista, 1971.
2. 'A History of the Avant-garde', cited in note 1.
3. See bibliography. Illustrated and discussed by John Willett in *The New Sobriety – Art and Politics in the Weimar Period, 1917–33*, Thames and Hudson, 1978.
4. The La Sarraz and Brussels conferences are documented in French by the special issue of *Travelling* (Cinémathèque Suisse), Summer 1979. Also see Peter Wollen, 'The Two Avant-Gardes', in *Readings and Writings*, New Left Books, 1982. Some recollections by S. M. Eisenstein can be found on pp. 134–7, *Immoral Memories*, Peter Owen, 1985.
5. 'A History of the Avant-garde', cited in note 1, p. 18.
6. See J. Willett (cited in note 3), p. 214 for details of similar film-making in the USSR by Piscator, Ivens and Eisler; also chap. 15, pp. 139–48, 'The camera eye; photography, Russian and avant garde films'. Brecht was working on the 'proletarian' film *Kuhle Wampe* at this time. Richter's

recollections of the *Metall* period can be found in *Hans Richter by Hans Richter*, ed. Cleve Gray, New York, 1971, pp. 44–7.

7. Werner Graeff's memoir in *Film as Film* (see note 1), p. 80, challenges some aspects of Richter's account of the early avant-garde. (Graeff, an associate of Richter's from the 1920s, wrote the accompanying volume to *Filmgegner* . . . for the 1929 'Film und Foto' exhibition: *Es kommt der neue Fotograf!* See: *Germany – The New Photography, Germany 1927–33*, ed. David Mellor, Arts Council, 1978.) Louise O'Konor has discussed the Richter–Eggeling issue at length in her *Viking Eggeling – Life and Work*, Stockholm, 1971.

8. Richter quotes Epstein on p. 60, and an even earlier reference to Canudo's formulation of 'photogénie' in 1911 on p. 119. For Epstein, see *Afterimage* 10, Autumn 1981 and *October* 3, Spring 1977.

9. 'The Author as Producer', in Walter Benjamin, *Understanding Brecht*, New Left Books, 1973. 'The Work of Art in the Age of Mechanical Reproduction' in Walter Benjamin, *Illuminations*, Jonathan Cape, 1970.

10. In 'The Work of Art . . .' see especially sections VIII–XIV. The quotation is from p. 239.

11. This is discussed by Ben Brewster in 'The Fundamental Reproach (Brecht)' *Ciné-tracts*, Vol 1, no. 2, Summer 1977, Canada.

12. See Chapter 1, Peter Wollen, *Signs and Meaning in the Cinema*, Secker and Warburg, 1972 (second edition).

13. For example, Richter refers to 'this "double" attitude that enables viewers to maintain their receptivity and even their capacity for working through even as they give in to the illusion (of film)', in a discussion of the spectator's response to both the realism and illusionism of cinema (p. 136).

14. Brecht's essays are in *New Left Review*, 84, March–April 1974, as 'Against Lukács' (reprinted with other relevant texts in *Aesthetics and Politics*, London, 1977). The events discussed here follow from the 1935 Paris meeting of the International Writers' Conference for the Defence of Culture' which supported socialist realism on Comintern lines. For a recent discussion of the alliance of Brecht, Benjamin and Bloch, see introduction by David Drew to Ernst Bloch, *Essays in the Philosophy of Music*, Cambridge, 1985. The Brecht quotation is from *New Left Review*, 84, p. 51.

15. Walter Benjamin, *Understanding Brecht* (see note 6), p. 116 ('Conversations with Brecht', July 1938 entries).

16. See 'Adorno-Benjamin Letters', *New Left Review*, 81, Sept.–Oct. 1973.

17. 'Adorno–Benjamin Letters', cited note 16, editorial introduction, p. 38.

18. See P. Adams Sitney, *Visionary Film – the American Avant-Garde 1943–78*, Oxford, 1974 and 1979; and editorial introduction to *The Avant-Garde Film: A Reader*, New York University Press, 1978.

19. I wish to thank Ben Brewster for kindly making available and allowing me to use his own background notes on *The Struggle for the Film*.

The Struggle for the Film

Gratefully dedicated to my wife, fellow-worker
and helpmate for thirty-five years
HANS RICHTER

Hans Richter.

Preface
by Jürgen Römhild

The Struggle for the Film was completed in manuscript by Hans Richter at the end of 1939.

No later than the shooting of *Metall* in 1933, Hans Richter had been on the National Socialists' blacklists in Germany. In February 1933, while he was still in Moscow working on the film, his house was sacked. He emigrated to France and made advertising documentaries for the Dutch firm Philips. In 1937, he was offered the post of head of production in the Zurich advertising film company Central-Film, and moved to Switzerland to take it up.

It was probably around this time that he began to write *The Struggle for the Film.*

The book was conceived in part as complementary to his work of 1929, *Enemies of Film Today – Friends of Film Tomorrow.* Whereas the latter had concentrated on questions of film aesthetics, *The Struggle for the Film* was concerned primarily to expound the cinema's social responsibility as a *mass medium* (by contrast with, say, painting!). On the other hand, it also represented a deliberate *prise de position* against totalitarian regimes such as that of the Third Reich – being written at a time when the Second World War had only just begun and its development, let alone its outcome, was not yet foreseeable.

The manuscript remained unpublished for thirty-five years. In 1941, Richter emigrated to the United States. Attempts to get it published there were unsuccessful.

The present version is about one third shorter than the original manuscript, an abridgement made with the consent – and indeed at the instigation – of Hans Richter himself, principally because of the way the cinema has developed since it was written. There was no intention, however, of in any way bringing the book up to date, of adapting it to the present situation. For much of what Richter wrote thirty-five years ago is as valid now as it was then – even if the 'cinema' in the sense in which it is described in this book no longer exists, having been replaced by television, which is only relatively comparable with the cinema, just as the cinema is only relatively comparable with the theatre.

Shortly before his death Hans Richter re-read the manuscript, added to it and polished it, with the result that the present text can be said to have his authorisation.

In editing the volume it was occasionally difficult to trace quotations to their sources; partly because Richter was a personal friend of nearly all the contemporaries he refers to and relied a great deal on his own notes and memories of conversations with them. But this is precisely one of the attractions of the book: its author witnessed and helped shape the history of the cinema overall.

I should like to thank all those whose help has enabled me to present the book in this form: above all Hans Richter and his wife, who answered all my questions very patiently and showed great consideration when the work went very slowly; but also all those who have helped me in other ways, like Werner Sudendorf of Munich and Mrs Pearl L. Moeller of the Museum of Modern Art in New York.

Introduction (Outline of contents)

PART ONE

Many books have been written about the cinema, and one can learn more or less everything from them about: the precise dating of cinematic developments; the artistic techniques of the different types of films; the technology of their manufacture and distribution; the artistic standards that have been evolved in the course of nearly eighty years of cinematic development; the mission the cinema should undertake; and many other things.

But much less has been written about the special forces that have encouraged and inhibited, influenced and diverted, accelerated or slowed down that development – in other words, about why and from where the cinema really derived its particular spirit and particular artistic, organisational, technological, political and economic, i.e., social form, and hence about its 'usefulness' to society.

But the answers to these questions are crucially important, for only those answers will tell us whether, despite its industrial manufacture, the cinema can develop in spirit as a free art like the other arts. The historiography of the cinema until now gives the impression that the cinema arose out of the encounter of certain artists with a new technology. But this will not do, for in no other art is the confluence of different social forces so influential on the spirit and form in which individual works are made as is the case with the cinema. Content and form are affected by the economy, by the political situation, by the level of technological development and by changes in public taste, as well as by artistic abilities.

These facts are well known, but the consequences for the historiography of the cinema or for the laws of film have rarely been drawn as yet – and the origins of the cinema, of its spirit and its form, have

23

hardly ever been examined in the light of the development of social forces.

Only the combined influence of these forces explains why the cinema has become what it is; and also what possibilities of future development it has – whether it is destined to a life of freedom or slavery, a living life or one constrained by forms of politico-economic coercion.

The question 'What is the cinema?' can only be answered properly if a second question is asked, too: 'What social purpose does the cinema serve?' Only in this context can we understand its artistic development as a whole and the development of each individual sector in every one of its forms.

How can this be done? On what conditions, and with what means? To answer such questions seems to me more important than ever in a period of mass persuasion and mass misleading like today.

I

But such questions are an extension of questions of aesthetics. The crisis, which now affects the arts, too, also signifies a crisis of idealist aesthetics. Lives and mores (i.e., men themselves) having been transformed, the ideas of this philosophy of the latest epoch of humanism must also be brought up to date. Given the threat of a general culture collapse, should the value of art continue to be measured exclusively according to aesthetic values intrinsic to art itself, or should it not rather also be assessed according to social standards external to it, an ethical 'use value'?

II

What is the cinema? How were and are the emergence of its spirit and form influenced by different social conditions, existing artistic traditions, technology, the economy, the political situation?

It is within this framework that the growth of the cinema will have to be examined. The cinema developed and perfected its technology on the basis of certain social needs. In doing so it drew on the weight of the artistic tradition of all the arts – but it also changed that tradition. In this way it grew step by step into an art, acquiring form and recreating it. The three kinds of film: 1) the documentary film, 2) the fantastic film (and the grotesque), and 3) the fiction film had each to break its own path, in conformity with its different technological and artistic, economic and social origins, and also in conformity with the social needs that allowed it to develop.

This concordance between an enormous social need (for relaxation, spectacle, knowledge and belief) and a new kind of technology and organisation thus gives a notion of the cinema's gigantic cultural, economic and social possibilities – and also raises the question of why these possibilities have been so little exploited.

III

The poor quality of most films is usually explained by the suggestion that the audience want bad films, so producers would be bankrupted if they refused to go along with this audience imperative, etc.

There can be no doubt that the mass audience greatly enjoy 'bad' films. But it can be doubted that this must exclusively be the case. Surely it is social conditions that keep the mass audience in a position in which they are unable even to develop the desire for anything else.

Poverty, hopelessness and poor education produce quite specific qualities in men. They encourage the need for 'inferior' spiritual sustenance – in the form of certain stereotypes – that will provide an appropriate anaesthetisation: for example, the preference to see wealth, the desire to do as little mental work as possible in the cinema, the pleasure obtained from moral and spiritual models that have long since been exposed as untrue, even, indeed, their admiration as ideals. These are among the symptoms of anyone who is exhausted.

Fortunately, however, such a summary diagnosis of the audience is inadequate. On the one hand, audiences are as diverse as our society itself; they contain in them positive and negative,

25

constructive and destructive, truth-seeking and truth-avoiding, progressive and reactionary forces. These different sections of the audience are capable of very different kinds of development, their deliberate reduction to a least common denominator in the cinema notwithstanding.

On the other hand, everyone is constantly receiving – in the street, in the office, in the underground – and also continuously working through. This capacity for working through is given nothing significant to do in the cinema.

Even if the audience in themselves were not such as to give the cinema a content and hence a higher level – is not the industry as a means of mass influence duty bound to do so, is it not its responsibility?

IV

Social values are no longer self-evident, no one believes in moral standards any more, but they do believe in the cinema – for the time being at least. Its suggestive power provides effective support for uncertain social values and even for moral standards that can be proved to have lost their validity today. It can be used to damp down progressive forces and to divert them into secondary channels. And it does so!

To support this – directly or indirectly, consciously or unconsciously – is not just a temptation for the film industry, it is an absolute necessity.

In this way, it cannot represent everyday life, for that would be to reveal the monstrous contradictions by which it is torn. It would itself be helping to undermine already uncertain social values to which it is committed. It therefore consistently seeks to present a 'rose-tinted' view of life, to romanticise it or completely traduce it. This is the *social mandate* it carries out.

The most important aspects of life are thus ruled out as representational content for the conventional cinema, with the result that it is restricted to areas of apparent social neutrality: eroticism, adventure, crime. As a result, what is allowed in the cinema is

Hans Richter (with scarf, left), S.M. Eisenstein (in policeman's
helmet), Len Lye (in hat, right), Basil Wright (in spectacles,
standing behind), with others, during the making of Richter's
Everyday in London in 1929.

becoming more and more devoid of content. But this puts the film industry in a dilemma.

It cannot and must not conform to those natural laws of development and extension that it ought to as an industry – cannot and must not exploit to the full the possibilities of the existing conjuncture. For who would dispute the fact that there is the conjuncture for other films, social ones with more content, touching everyone's vital interests? Precisely to touch those vital interests, however, would be to do further damage to the already shaky foundations of society. Moreover, the contradictions within the audience itself would be aggravated and the audience split, whereas film production needs precisely a unitary audience.

The problems of the age force the industry to take a position – but this is exactly what it wants above all to avoid doing. It does not want to take sides and yet it does so, it wants to be neutral and yet it is drawn into social controversies which damage its business.

Thus it is between the devil and the deep blue sea, and its products are not just the 'chosen diet' of an audience that 'wants' to see bad films, but also the result of its own contradictory situation.

Nevertheless, alongside and inside this film industry works are produced in which a progressive spirit is detectable. Whether this *other spirit* arises within the official cinema or represents rather another line of development distinct from that of the official cinema will be investigated in the second part of this book.

PART TWO

V

The history of the cinema is usually written as if there was an art of film developing with a single inspiration. Closer examination reveals, however, that this presupposition is untenable.

The divergence of inspirations within society naturally finds an expression in the cinema. To write the history of the cinema as if it was borne by a unitary cultural will has long been a disputable enterprise. Today such a historiography of the art of film can only serve to confuse, not to clarify.

Purely formal evaluations are no longer sufficient. In theoretical and aesthetic judgements, too, a decision must be made for or against the prolongation of what is left of the cultural heritage: or else one will have to go on speaking of perfect artistic form even when one is forced to admit that the object which has obtained that form is no more than a 'wax-works ideal'.

The history of the cinema, like that of society, is split into two divergent lines. As a result, the progressive cinema can no longer be identified simply with the artistic cinema. On 'the other side', too, there are masterpieces of technico-artistic form. The history of the progressive cinema is rather that of the European spirit trying to obtain some kind of self-consciousness and hence a tradition of its own in this art too.

This history spans the works of Flaherty and Pabst, Dulac and Wiene, Capra and Eisenstein, Chaplin, René Clair and others, from mere uncommited depiction of a milieu, via the depiction of mores, social criticism and accusation to the knowledge of a new social content. This development shows that those striving for civilisation in Europe and America do see an aim and a content in the cinema, too – an aim and a content that can in no way be brought into harmony with those of the official cinema, and are detaching themselves from the latter as proof of the development of a new humanist inspiration.

VI

Building on the experiences of progressive cinema, on the survey provided in Chapter V, Chapter VI will attempt to make those experiences applicable in a dramaturgy of progressive cinema – within the common denominator: the audience in the cinema too should be encouraged to pay attention, compare and think.

The official cinema has a highly developed dramaturgy of tested effectivity. But these effects and means are components of a system that aims to make even a film without 'content' acceptable and pleasurable.

However, a dramaturgy intended to awaken in the audience an interest in the complexities of life, to contribute to an interpretation of life in the cinema rather than its concealment, a dramaturgy intended not just to fascinate the audience but also to interest it in the content itself – such a dramaturgy will necessarily have to overhaul the tested methods of the official cinema, to change them or develop them to its own ends.

It must seek such dramaturgical forms as will make an audience that is reluctant to think do precisely that, with ease and without loss of pleasure, such forms as will raise their general, moral and spiritual receptivity, and will constantly evade, break out of and pierce the bounds at present set to speaking the truth.

Whether this aim is attained by a skilful presentation of facts (in the documentary film) or in the manner of the fool who speaks the truth (in the grotesque) or with great pathos (in the fiction film), a changing cinematic dramaturgy will increasingly be able to find its guidelines in this growing sense of responsibility.

The development which has taken place within the framework of the official cinema also provides us with many examples of this, examples whose significance has hitherto been almost impossible to demonstrate simply because the movement they represented had as yet no name and seemed no more than an oppositional variant of that official cinema.

Only when this has become quite clear is it worth investigating the means of expression and forms, too (those of the actor as well as of the sets, of the editing as well as the dialogue); only then can one analyse their significance and appropriateness as the bearers of an intellectual and artistic development.

VII

As bearer of the content and embodiment of the ideas in the cinema, the actor carries an essential part of the responsibility for its development.

The antagonisms dividing present-day society are also detectable in acting styles, for the actor has to model men – but the spirit to be breathed into those men, their style of behaviour, the interpretation to be given to the writer's words and characters, are prescribed to the actor by the period and the society in which he lives; and in so far as he performs his tasks in conformity with his period, he is also taking up a position towards the ideas at work in that period and society.

On the stage, and even more on the screen, yesterday's man in yesterday's period survives in countless tried and tested plays, scenes, feelings, nuances, modes of expression.

The new man emerging today can only be made to prevail in opposition to the old. And this is not just a question of subject matter, it is also one of acting style. The new style derives from a changed attitude on the actor's part to the content of his performance.

The actor is above all a modeller of men, and it is the intensity with which he is able to endow the men he acts on stage or screen that brings them to life – but does it bring the content, too, to life?

The intoxicatory presentation of characters on the stage and screen is familiar enough: we are hypnotised, or asked to admire the acting skill 'in itself'. We are seduced into sympathising with the people in these plays and films for their own sakes. Jannings shows us Tartuffe as a clinical case, as a scurrilous individual. But what is the meaning of Tartuffe? Did Molière give him no other, no socially more significant meaning?

A new balance between the representation of men and the presentation of ideas on stage and screen: to bring ideas to life without detriment to the living human character of the figures – on the contrary, to extend that human character beyond the merely individualistic. If the actor can carry out this task, he will win the audience for the pleasure there is in knowledge, and hence have a more profound, a redoubled influence.

VIII

Actors are the most important means of expression in the cinema; like them, the other means, too, are drawn into the ongoing conflict between yesterday and tomorrow.

Works which lack any content other than that of entertainment have to be provided with more accessories (scenery, etc.) than those that use scenery, frame composition, sequential organisation, editing and dialogue to make a meaning clear.

The development of the cinema may only just have begun, but some things have already been forgotten, and the latest invention is by no means always the most modern.

The wealth of means of expression, the refinement of the technology have made the audience very demanding. The less meaning there is in the cinema, the more necessary it becomes to bribe them at the formal level.

Set design, individual shot structure, editing and dialogue are only apparently the same in an obscurantist and an enlightening cinema. They too represent methods by which to help make a content clear. In the conventional cinema they are often only one-sidely developed, certain developmental possibilities being neglected because, for example, they are ill-adapted to a repertoire devoted primarily to romanticisation. But they may perhaps come into their own tomorrow, when methods are needed for tearing off the veils.

Technology itself, of course, is constantly advancing, and the technology of 1905 can no longer be revived in the contemporary film; artistic methods, on the other hand, appear and disappear again, and with new artists and in a new form they can regain a new significance.

Artistic technique, too, is determined by its content, and that content by the cultural consciousness – or lack of consciousness – of the creator.

Whoever loves the cinema should defend it, to prevent every individual's right to the cinema being completely swallowed up by commercial interests.

Only then will it be possible for films of progressive inspiration, of any inspiration at all, to prevail; only then will we see in the cinema not just films that are better or worse propaganda; only in this way can the cinema participate creatively in the life of society and thus demonstrate its justification to existence as an art.

Whether this will happen depends on whether society is able to preserve the very freedoms without which the cinema, too, cannot live.

Part One
The cinema as a product of the twentieth century

Bertolt Brecht.

I. Art as a social need

In 1926, one of the then biggest German industrialists, well known as a friend of science and the arts, commissioned for a recently established housing estate for his employees a bronze sculpture – a giant stag by August Gaul.

Where the main square of the estate was to be, a plinth was built, cranes were set up and the sculpture carefully winched into place.

The donor ceremonially presented it to a gathering of the employees with a few well-intentioned words about the significance of art, how it refines our sensibilities and helps us lift ourselves above the everyday round.

The newspapers praised the work. The art critics found clever ways to eulogise it.

The next morning, the five-ton stag had been pushed over.

The factory management were surprised and annoyed at this wicked act of juvenile vandalism. They had the stag put up again.

The stag was pushed over once again, and once again replaced. This time, however, two guards were left to keep watch over it.

The next morning the guards had been beaten up and the stag was on the ground again.

This was going too far. The magnanimous donor was not just annoyed, he could not understand what motive anyone could have for such barbarous hostility to his gift; especially given that his relations with his employees were by no means particularly tense.

When, not long afterwards, he accidentally overheard the stubborn explanation 'What use have we for a stag?', he was so hurt by this lack of insight that he took up the cudgels again.

In order to prevent the barbaric behaviour of a few philistines winning a victory over good taste, he had the stag put up again and surrounded by a thirty-foot-high barbed-wire fence.

This time the work of art remained standing.

35

The main motive behind the events described is no doubt to be sought in economic and political differences. The bitterness of the conflict was determined by the bitterness of the social struggle running alongside it.

However, political and social explanations of the events are hardly sufficient in themselves. Had a sculpture by Constantin Meunier such as 'Grieving Mother' or 'Miner' been set up instead of the stag, we can be sure no one would have attacked it. The workers' hostility was directed against this particular object.

What was at stake was the rejection of an art in which they found nothing expressed that corresponded to their own vital interests. Their opposition was aroused by the glaring discrepancy between (perfect) form and (to them irrelevant) content. They demanded first of all a content corresponding to their situation. Only in relation to such a content could they assess the value of the form, the artistic value, not vice versa; they had neither the specialised education nor the leisure necessary for such a study of the arts. So they saw (if at all) a perfect form and a content completely irrelevant to them put on show in a particularly visible and prestigious place.

As a result, the stag became for them a symbol of a useless and exaggerated concern for form and beauty; they saw it as a provocation, because they had other, more urgent needs – including needs of an artistic kind.

Someone who judges in this way has no notion of separating enjoyment of form from that of content. He is interested primarily in the content and his instinctive wish is to get something useful out of the enjoyment of art. The content provides this. A century earlier, if anyone would have dared pull a stunt like this, it would have been drunken students. A gang who inflicted such indignities on a bronze statue would certainly have had to deal with the workers themselves at the second attempt. The very persistence of the action on this occasion reveals the profundity of the spiritual transformations taking place in this society. These workers attacking a stag constitute an example of the extent to which art is in crisis as a social factor.

But does it mean that there has been a crisis in the concepts of art in general? Have the concepts that idealist philosophical thinkers proposed for art and its appreciation lost their validity today? Have the profound changes in our conditions of existence and our society, including its morality and ethos, produced a corresponding change in our aesthetic views?

Is art perhaps not so free and independent of material intentions as Schopenhauer supposed? Could it be that 'interest' should have something to say in the enjoyment of art, that it should obtain some satisfaction from it? Could it be that art and its enjoyment are not completely cut off from daily life, not the pure forgetfulness of self and recall of higher things that those thinkers held them to be? Could they also be the self-recall of daily life (or its justified inability to forget itself), in Lessing's sense?

To bring together these questions of art and of the social needs it satisfies has always been a major problem of aesthetics and one that divides opinion.

Today, now that the cinema, radio and television affect millions of people, the question is of correspondingly greater practical importance.

However inadmissible it may be to try to subordinate knowledge to transient needs, in the last analysis it must be asked whether an art remains an art if there is hardly anyone left who has access to it, or is capable of assimilating and enjoying it. In other words, whether the social value of art should be introduced into aesthetics as a partially determinant factor. Arnheim's assertion[1] that one *Student Prince* has more artistic value than all the 'proletarian' films put together, however curious, is perfectly compatible with the rules of contemporary aesthetics. But it means nothing less than that a piece of humbug that Lubitsch has given some artistic life to is more valuable than any less perfect film, even if the latter's content is closer to reality.

Such a statement from the profoundest film theoretician of his day demonstrates the contradiction that has spread to aesthetics and hence to the artistic judgements based on it as a result of the process of social transformation.

The director who commissioned the stag could certainly appeal to his knowledge of the essence of art and artistic taste as elaborated by idealist philosophy, but the employees, too, were entitled to assert their right to demand an art that did not refuse them that interpretation of life that they needed and awaited.

Is it good enough that criticism not forget the freedom of art if this strict observance turns artistic appreciation into a kind of hermeticism separating art from its social meaning? A situation has arisen which is getting more and more acute and makes it difficult to maintain the concept of art as an absolute over and against the practice of life.

The notion of man as an isolated ego, a being definable in himself alone, is proving less fruitful than ever today. The image of man in the sense of late humanism is proving more and more in need of the complementary image of a socially conditioned man. Man can no longer be posited as absolute and invariant.

It is precisely our knowledge of the possible freedom of art that allows us to speak of its factual unfreedom, its constraint. It is free only in an absolute sense. At the same time, however, constrained. Only in a balance between its absolute freedom and its transient constraint can it discover its form.

An art which is no longer accessible makes nonsense of the notion of the freedom of art. The conditions under which a (free) art can be appreciated are a component part of that art, as are the social and material conditions amidst which the artist grows up, lives and creates. They constitute a part of his ego, and he is determined by them, just as he is by his period, the society in which he lives and the prejudices that it gives rise to. A 'free' individual – in the sense above – is no more possible than an art guided by the needs of the world in which it appears.

Hence the needs of society for an art and the content of that art are interconnected, and the stormier the period, the closer the connection.

A recognition of the absolute value of art as an expression of the freedom of the human spirit must not be equated with the artist's lack of social responsibility. The investigation that follows seeks to help explain how far the social problems we are confronted with by the revolutionary character of our period, and not least the technology that makes it possible to speak to billions every day via the cinema, radio and television, affect and change the basic theses of the aesthetics we have grown up with.

It is the age of technology that has produced the cinema, and the latter has grown together with the needs it satisfies. But a whole series of different factors had to come together for the cinema to be possible.

The cinema is the product of a highly developed, ultra-highly specialised technology, not the invention of one individual. It is the result of the intersection of many inventions. Its development required a particular mode of production: the industrial mode of production. Only the latter enabled it to fulfil its historic task: to reach the masses and to reach them everywhere. For the industrial mode of production is the first to need a very broad field of operations: the whole world as the market for its products.

And again: as industry developed, it needed more and more labourers, giving rise to vast accumulations of proletarians in overcrowded industrial zones. These masses lacked appropriate places of entertainment, and the cinema met their aesthetic demands, their desire for spectacle, entertainment and instruction. No sooner had film been invented and discovered than it became, thanks to its easy reproducibility, the 'theatre for the masses'.

In this fact lies the responsibility that the cinema owes to the masses who entrust themselves to it. They believe it: it is a power, and because it is a power, the different forces of our period are struggling with one another to control it, to infiltrate it and to lend it their coloration.

As a result, the cinema is less 'free' than any other art. Hence the direction in which it develops cannot be deduced simply from the artistic personalities who bring about its advances and the peculiarities of its technology – less even than with any other art.

What audiences see on the screen every evening and like to admire as 'art' is determined by many different factors: by individual creativity; by the artistic traditions of the older arts; by the evolutionary drive of technology; by the material and ideal limits of the industry; by the audience's leanings, which vary according to periods, conditions of life and classes; by the contemporary social situation; by artistic, economic, social and political crises; and by the contradictions that coexist in an epoch in which greater progress has been made in the domination of nature than in millennia hitherto – such rapid progress that ideas, habits, and institutions have not had time to catch up.

II. Rise

THE DOCUMENTARY FILM

In 1923, a Jew emigrated to Palestine. He had few possessions, only an old film projector and a single ancient film. With these he installed himself in the poorest Arab quarter of Jerusalem. His film ran for several months. The audience never failed him; indeed, he noticed many faces that returned again and again.

One day by mistake the last reel was run first. Surprisingly, there were no complaints. Even the 'regulars' failed to stir. This intrigued the cinema owner. He wanted to find out if anyone objected, and if not why not, so he ran all the reels in any order. No one seemed to mind. 'Why?', he wondered in some amazement, and asked one of his oldest customers. It turned out that the Arabs had never grasped the plot, even when the film was shown in the right order. It was clear that they only went to the cinema because there one could see people walking, horses galloping, dogs running.

The visitors to the Lumières' film cellar in 1895 were probably only interested in this one aspect, too. They were amazed by the magical technology, captivated by the fact that things moved, and overjoyed to recognise the simplest events.

For the first time man contemplated his image in motion – objectively, as something alien. This was the *primal cinema*!

People were astonished by something they had seen a thousand times, workers streaming out of a factory, say. They were amazed at the way men's trouser legs went up and down as they walked, they applauded the ordinary traffic in the Boulevard des Italiens – in a moving picture – and would go again and again to see the 'Arrival of a Train at La Ciotat Station', arrivals of trains at any station in the world, the mere sight of turning wheels.

It was as if the movement of things – of the surrounding world –

of oneself had been discovered for the first time. The sheet hanging at the other end of the room provided a plane on which one could examine things as if they were on another planet and oneself an alien being.

This experience was provided us by modern technology. In the beginning it was the technology that was admired, as when the radio first appeared. The first enthusiastic radio fans, too, were originally quite indifferent to the quality of radio transmissions. Fascination with the curious technology and delight at every recognisable squawk initially overshadowed any artistic expectations.

Or as in the earliest days of the sound cinema: Henny Porten's first talkie achieved its greatest success not in the actress's performance but with the astonishingly genuine-sounding pop of a champagne cork![2]

While the shots of the Boulevard des Italiens and of workers leaving the Lumière factory were fascinating simply because it was possible to recognise moving objects in them, the pictures in *Fire at the Charity Bazaar*, *Unter den Linden* and *The Tsar's Arrival in Paris* were already guiding this interest into a new direction. No longer was it moving trouser legs and turning wheels that were interesting, no longer the simple fact, but the *contemporary historical fact*.

Technology, overcoming time and space, has brought all life on earth so close together that the most remote 'facts', as much as those closest to hand, have become significant for each individual's life. Reason has given rise to a secularisation of the divine. Everything that happens on earth has become more interesting and more significant than it ever was before. Our age demands the documented fact.

Intercine writes: 'Idealistic historiographers have used gallons of ink to demonstrate that "documentaries", even in historical subjects, have only such value as derives from the mind which interprets them. Today, on the contrary, the document seems to aim at invading the field of philosophic history, as well as artistic emotion. Everything seems "documentary". Roughly speaking, we can attribute this character especially to works in which a creative personality obstinately disguises and hides itself to obtain a better *pretence* or *fiction* of objective reality; to trick out the plot with a subtler artifice.'[3]

The character of the epoch provides the explanation for this: as a result of the monstrous division of labour, the individual is in danger of losing any overview. But the more rationalised the working life of the individual today, the greater is his need to see something other than parts for once, to grasp connections for once.

Magazine reportage has long been unable to satisfy the curiosity for 'facts'. The modern reproductive technology of the cinematograph was uniquely responsive to the need for factual sustenance. The (apparent) incorruptibility of optics guaranteed 'absolute truth'. From the workers leaving the Lumière factory via the Tsar's trip to Paris to the images of First-World-War destruction: facts are represented everywhere – and facts are the soil from which history grows.

In its second stage the primal cinema was presented with the social task of gathering facts, of documenting them, and the meaning of the document was the reality to which it so precisely cleaved.

In this first stage of the *documentary film* it is only an accident when the images have an artistic form. The new technology presented enough difficulties and problems to occupy the makers of such films. Understandably, there was little pressure to add to one's difficulties for aesthetic reasons; there was hardly any scope for the emergence of a need to make what was represented more expressive by organising it artistically. For a start, the audience, too, were quite satisfied with straight reproduction so long as it fulfilled the ideal of the most exact reproduction possible. Thus the documentary film was confronted with vast quantities of untouched material. It could be all the more confident of the audience's intensive interest in so far as the image (and especially the moving image) with its intuitive character, corresponded ideally to the masses' receptivity, better than the newspapers, for in comparison with words, images make relatively low demands on one's powers of abstraction.

Hence it was only natural that in its earliest stage the documentary film made no attempt to distinguish between subject matter and form; rather it sought to extend the former as widely as possible. When familiar facts (workers leaving a factory, the Tsar's trip, etc.) were no longer enough to satisfy the interest in the present, there were countless unfamiliar facts that could be reproduced: zoological themes, ethnological themes, and so on.

The camera created a reservoir of human observation, in the simplest possible way.

Stage Two: Beauty

But even the most thoughtless and primitively shot reproductions are often attractive, and it was quickly realised what images – over and above their content – exerted this attraction on the audience: the glimmer of a sunset, silhouettes of wind-tossed blades of grass. . . . The new technology provided new 'beauties' which the masses had never dreamed of before.

Audiences as well as film-makers were fascinated by the possibility of obtaining 'beauty' from moving photographs. As well as the possibility of shaping facts, the temptation appeared of giving the image an extra aesthetic attractiveness. This stage of the factual film represented the first step towards an artistic form.

But this was significant in another respect, too: the 'beautiful picture' marked the cinema's first direct overtures to the artistic climate of the period – to the tradition of the bourgeois arts.

Hitherto a purely technological way of reproducing facts, the cinema now began to loosen, to modify this purely mechanical mandate. It began to seek models of beauty, grace, light and value where they were ideally to be found: in the fine arts.

These arts had a long and tested tradition: one could learn what was 'beautiful' from them. The cinema could borrow their 'beauty', embellish itself and hope perhaps one day to be able to compete with these related arts.

So mood was manufactured with soft-focus lenses, obtrusive contrasts were reduced with gauzes and gratings, and natural objects were transformed into romantic or impressionist paintings. Details could be retouched, highlights diffused, outlines smudged. The cinema took over painting – and the poetry of the painted image took over the cinema.

44

The film image attempted to imitate the oil painting, to take over its beauty without any concern for its tradition. For in painting the world of appearances had found its formal expression, its perfection, its meaning, its standard and its supreme beauty. So why not apply the finished article as a recipe? This period produced such films as *A Castle on the Rhine, Chicago Stockyards, Building an Aircraft, War in China* and *Exhibition of Rare Flowers,* all photographed with the same concern to look 'beautiful'.

However, the application of the recipe did not produce the desired result. It had been assumed that this embellishment of the image would increase the audience's attraction. But this did not happen – at least not for long. The audience were much less receptive to the most beautiful moods than had been hoped; pictures on the screen that were no more than beautiful soon became boring, and they debased the cinema into a kind of extension of the picture postcard.

The 'beauty' and the rules of expression produced by painting are not just forms, they are the bearers of a determinate social content. Painting is directed at a different group of spectators from the cinema's. It is as exclusive as the theatre.

The unpretentious freshness the documentary film had brought to film art by the exact reproduction of facts, the impetus the audience's interest in real facts had given it were to a degree dissipated by this 'embellishing' representation.

Hitherto the cinema had grown out of its own resources. Contact with the old arts, however, reduced its impetus, for their origins, aims and spirit were not for it. As documentary film, the cinema will and must get to the facts, whereas the painted picture lives in a cultural sphere of its own, and in our period has such specialised tasks that it hardly comes into contact with that of the cinema. And yet the cinema had first to learn more from painting, for just as the fine arts are an expression of our aesthetic ideas, so the factual film could only attain to a formal organisation by settling accounts with the existing tradition of painting. But certain facts, and precisely the most important ones, are in contradiction with a general, smoothing embellishment.

It became clear that a fact did not really remain a 'fact' if it appeared in too beautiful a light. The accent shifted, for a 'beautiful' image could not normally be obtained except at the expense of its closeness to reality. Something essential had to be suppressed in order to provide a beautiful appearance. Hence contact with the tradition of painting proved dangerous. This contradiction between beautiful form and social task, i.e., the task of representing historical facts, marked the cinema in this stage of its development.

The Beautiful Village and the True Village

How is a documentary normally (if not ideally) produced?

A film team is commissioned to go somewhere where, for whatever reason, the commissioner hopes to obtain something. When they arrive, they shoot what they find beautiful, attractive, well lit, picturesque. I once saw such a 'normal' film: pictures from a Southern European mountain landscape. . . .

– From the top of a pass, over a grove of stunted oaks, a village is visible on the mountain slopes, very romantic in its construction. Picturesque country roads, massive antique stone bridges, a dry stream bed, fields laid out in terraces, and so on. A ragged muleteer, a peasant harrowing his field with a drawn board come into view. These serious figures seem to live there uniformly, according to the 'eternal laws of the earth', far from the restlessness and anxiety of the city.

A year later, I was on holiday in the same region, and I learnt to see the same beauties with new eyes.

The film had carefully avoided anything which might have disturbed the pleasant impression. It was no documentation of that village but an anthology of all its 'beauties' that had been filmed.

At an earlier period the inhabitants had lived almost exclusively by smuggling. When the border shifted after the War, they lost this means of livelihood. Most of the men emigrated, leaving their families behind. There were blood feuds with the neighbouring villages, the drawn board was a sign of unimaginable poverty, the harmonious silence signified depopulation and flight from a wilderness.

Outwardly everything looked quite picturesque, and there were plenty of opportunities for marvellous shots. But such a manner teaches one nothing about the object represented. And yet this is the 'documentarist's' usual style, this superficial reportage. The task of the documentary film is, on the contrary, to make such a village understandable in its functions, too, i.e., socially, not just as a beautiful landscape. Only in this way can the true face, an authentic picture of how men live together, be produced.

However, because such a practice is the norm, audiences have rightly become very suspicious of the merely 'beautiful'. All too often the beautiful form has been chosen to conceal the reality, to falsify it, to blind the spectator to what is essential. But it is more sensible to renounce external 'beauty' than the truth, than the communication of the facts. For the 'beautiful', too, is more likely to emerge as an attribute of the truth than the truth is as an attribute of the 'beautiful'.

'As a result, the situation is becoming so complex that less than ever does a simple reproduction of reality tell us anything about reality. A photograph of Krupps or the AEG yields hardly anything about those industries. True reality has taken refuge in the functional.'

(Bertolt Brecht)[4]

If the forces that determine men's destinies today have become anonymous, so too has their appearance. Hence we are obliged to look behind the façade – if facts are to be revealed.

The cinema is perfectly capable in principle of revealing the *functional* meaning of things and events, for it has *time* at its disposal, it can contract it and thus show the development, the evolution of things. It does not need to take a picture of a 'beautiful' tree, it can also show us a growing one, a falling one, or one swaying in the wind – nature not just as a view, but also as an element, the village not as an idyll, but as a social entity.

The documentary film can therefore contribute to a knowledge of the true conditions – of life.

Flaherty was the first to use the documentary film in order to give modern men what really interests them about the document. He brought out the meaning of the facts, 'interpreted' them.

His film *Nanook of the North* reveals man's attitude to his environment, his self-assertion in the most difficult conditions of life – those of permanent ice.

This is no series of pretty shots, however pretty and picturesque some of them may be, it provides insight into the lives of these people. The factual film is fulfilling its task when it represents these conditions in their overall structure. To be documentary means to seek out and present the social problems in the subject matter, to subordinate all the reproduction to that aim.

Of course, Flaherty's films usually remain on the periphery of what we are concerned with in social life today. His *Man of Aran*, *Nanook*, *Moana* deal with problems that are exotically and romantically remote from the vast majority of cinema-goers; civilisation's struggle with nature is of less importance to them, it shrinks into insignificance in comparison with social problems afflicting them much closer to home. Nevertheless, the methods and techniques of the documentary film as created by Flaherty are still exemplary today.

Revolutionary Technology

Everyone comes into contact with technology today. This has given rise to a general interest in how things work: beginning with the curiosity aroused by the workings of the earliest cinematographic machines, it extends to a general pleasure in the operations and purposes of more complex machines.

This interest is also in evidence in a metaphorical sense: people are eager to know how things are put together, how they look, what effects they have on one another. Technology is as close to society today as nature. As a result, people demand to see themselves and 'their' technology.

The (historically conditioned) mistake of the documentary film was its overestimation of a traditional notion of 'beauty'. 'How things work' in life was neglected.

For what a world is opened to us when a film shows us the growth of a leaf of grass or a salt crystal, or the composition of a drop of water. We experience the technology of mechanical connections, our mental powers are brought into play in proportion to our aesthetic emotions – we demonstrate interest.

The technology of scientific cinematography (slow motion, fast motion, microcinematography, etc.) was not originally expected to be aesthetically attractive, but it chimes with the audience's fascination with the aesthetics of technology – notwithstanding the fact that this technology distorts reality. Against conventional truth to nature, against the aesthetic rules inherited from painting, the cinema has created a means of expression of its own with a qualitatively different persuasive power because it no longer merely copies its objects but analyses them while and by copying them.

If Flaherty in his epics still made little use of the camera's many technical possibilities, they provided Vertov with a basis for extemporisation. Using his camera and all the possibilities of the lens and the printer, he rearranged and distorted the facts – where Flaherty had collected and presented them by patient observation – and for the same purpose, in order to achieve an interpretation of the neutral facts.

Vertov stuck more strictly to the facts themselves than Flaherty, he did not look for romanticism, rather for everyday life. He avoided any narrative thread, any posed or reconstructed picture. Vertov built up a network of contacts and was on the spot with his camera: he collected documents.

The incorruptibility of his representation of real life remains unsurpassed. But it was also needed. The representation of reality was all the more important to the masses in Russia at that time in so far as that reality was undergoing an extraordinary transformation.

Vertov's shots had the character of news, but in quite a different way from a conventional newsreel. His documents were seen from the people's viewpoint, they showed everyday life, ordinary people. He took selected *'faits divers'* from the new everyday life of his country, the Soviet Union, every incident from birth to death, and attempted, without the assistance of a unitary time or space, just in disconnected factual fragments, to attain a social interpretation nonetheless. If Vertov's shots themselves hardly went beyond the stage of the primal cinema (i.e., the pure fixation of facts), his method of stringing together the pieces he had obtained in such a primitive way enabled him to make a momentous step forward. That is, the fact that he rejected every plot as something in contradiction with documentary film, yet for that reason had to face the difficulty of finding a framework for his multitudes of unconnected scenes. Splicing them together at random produced a crazy chaos of mutually interfering episodes. The more he investigated the causes of this interference, the more he realised that every image, every scene, every shot had its own, as it were, musical rhythm of motion, which, if it was not organised, emerged as interference. Whenever it so happened, on the contrary, that compatible rhythms of motion accidentally came together, the image 'chimed' and something comparable to a melody emerged.

Vertov studied the motion of the material photographed according to the length, tempo and type of its emotional and dynamic quality. He eventually succeeded (on the basis of such investigations) in composing rhythmically with image motions.

Thus where there were no 'threads' in the content, he created them by rhythmic combination.

Thus Vertov located the expressiveness of the object photographed in the expressiveness of its movement. Faces, trees, clouds, a falling drop of blood became, in the rhythm of Vertov's series of images, a metrical language of the document – became *film poetry*.

To the objection that his films contained no intellectual unity, Vertov replied that, once one had discovered the rhythm they contain and could link the parts together like passages of notes, the thousands of facts brought together yielded an overall melody

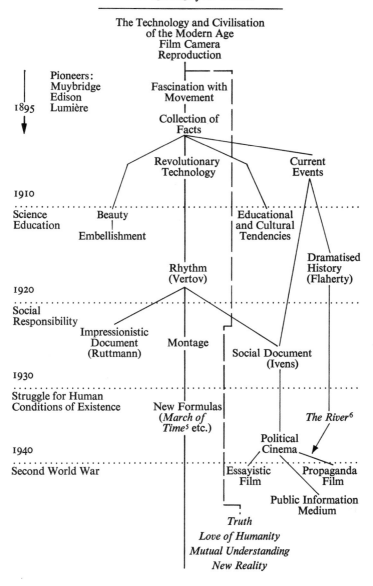

The Technology and Civilisation
of the Modern Age
Film Camera
Reproduction

Pioneers:
Muybridge
Edison
Lumière

1895

Fascination with
Movement

Collection of
Facts

Revolutionary
Technology

Current
Events

1910

Science
Education

Beauty

Embellishment

Educational
and Cultural
Tendencies

Dramatised
History
(Flaherty)

Rhythm
(Vertov)

1920

Social
Responsibility

Impressionistic
Document
(Ruttmann)

Montage

Social Document
(Ivens)

1930

Struggle for Human
Conditions of Existence

New Formulas
(*March of
Time*[5] etc.)

The River[6]

Political
Cinema

1940

Second World War

Essayistic
Film

Propaganda
Film

Public Information
Medium

Truth
Love of Humanity
Mutual Understanding
New Reality

51

which, together with the concrete content of the scenes, should reveal the meaning of the work.*

The silent rhythm of shot sequences, most thoroughly exploited in Russian silent films especially, derives from Vertov. By the organisation of movements into an overall rhythm, he raised the cinematic fact to the level of free artistic elaboration.

As in the primal cinema, the fact remained a fact; but mere reproduction had been overcome, a style had been born, the artistic possibilities of the documentary film had been established once and for all.

From Flaherty and Vertov to Ruttmann and Ivens, to Vigo and Kaufman, to Cavalcanti and Richter, to the English, Dutch and Swiss groups, the Belgian group around Storck, the brilliant Russian documentarist Turin and the Americans, the development of the documentary film has made it into a social document of our age.

The significance of the documentary film will increase to the extent that people grow more interested in the knowledge of reality. For we learn far more about ourselves from the documentary film, if its makers are capable of following people's social behaviour, than we do from the fiction film, in which the characters must always be more concerned to appear as the ruling ideal says they should than as they really are. The documentary film has drawn concrete life back into the circle of art and thus cleared the ground for a knowledge of the interconnections of life.

THE FANTASTIC FILM

The official evolution of cinematography has taken place in the fiction film. The latter (for reasons I shall discuss later) has

* In the same period, Viking Eggeling and the author were working on the same problem of musical rhythm in film. Quite like Vertov, we studied rhythm as the central problem of film composition – a notion that later became one of the most essential foundations of the international avant-garde cinema movement.

evolved on a much broader scale than its two older brothers, the documentary and the fantastic film.

If it is the job of the documentary film to be 'true', the fantastic film has the task of confounding reality, distorting it, changing it at the behest of fantasy, or merely hinting at it, as if through a fog – allowing the impossible and the nonsensical to become visible.

The most 'primitive' cinematic field is that of the fantastic film (or the grotesque film). Its forebears are thoroughly unpresentable: the fairground, the waxworks museum, the conjuring display and the circus. It has no models in any of the arts and to that extent it has no aesthetic tradition, it is not bound to a form that has existed for centuries.

But precisely this extraction is its advantage: for a start, the cinema by no means suffers if the language it speaks is a 'vulgar' one. The people understand that language, the fairground and the circus have made it familiar to them. As a result they feel at home with it.

In the earliest days of the cinema, a good thirty per cent of films represented such 'popular offerings'. At that time, the cinema itself was a fairground entertainment and its producers were showmen and conjurers like Georges Méliès.

Thanks to his lack of prejudices and inhibitions, Méliès, the father of the fantastic film, was the first to unlock the secret powers of the camera. He took his cue from the technical potentialities of the camera and of film, in which there were a thousand different discoveries waiting to be made, each having a dozen different possibilities of development. Méliès realised this and began to develop these possibilities from the first moments of his activity.

Méliès used the camera as a conjuring machine. He invented the miracle for the cinema. If the documentary film was concerned with objective reality, with the most precise, even microscopic reproduction, Méliès treated the world of objects and facts as no more than a pretext – to transform them.

Most camera tricks were discovered at this time. Some of them have since been forgotten, for they are hardly used any more today. But then, when the fifteen short films in a programme included at least five fantastic films or magical grotesques, making films really meant being able to conjure with the camera.

But Méliès too had certain traditional connections, with the theatre and with painting. The world in which his films took place was the set of his *Théâtre Robert Houdin*.[7] But that set was no longer a flat surface *in front of* which conjuring tricks were performed, it was a *space*. The naivety of the decors reminds one of the Douanier Rousseau, their romanticism of Delacroix, whose powerful frames Méliès broke by having the shadows of real clouds pass over Delacroix's romantic canvases.

The obviously cardboard walls were no more an obstacle to the illusion than a complete lack of scenery had been in Shakespeare's day. However technically feeble the settings, the miraculous infected them with its fiery spirit. No one complained that the walls shook in the bedroom where an uncanny spirit persistently tried to pull the bedclothes from a sleeping woman.

What is amazing about Méliès – given the extraordinarily primitive character of his technology – is the unity of decor, actors and staging. Neither actors nor decors are particularly outstanding in themselves, although the latter often demonstrate the fertility of Méliès' imagination. But the unity of cinematic form and expression that Méliès had attained by 1900 was only equalled by the fiction film much later.

In Méliès' films, as in Disney's later, the decor had become an active character, a participating component, alongside the human beings.

But actors, too, were for him no more than objects by means of which he could attain the miraculous world of the fairy tale. The true actor remained the camera.

'What might, for the fiction film, for
naturalistic reproduction, be called the
"drawbacks" of film technique (which
technicians are doing their best to
overcome) in reality form the tools of
the creative artist.' (Arnheim)[8]

A thief is clapped into gaol. Hardly have the gaolers left him than he escapes, simply by walking through the bars as if they were made of some penetrable material. Unfortunately, he is caught again and locked into the cell. This time, however, he is put in ankle irons which are chained to the wall. Don't imagine that this is a serious obstacle to his flight! A close-up shows how first one foot, then the other unscrew themselves, move miraculously away from the trouser leg and walk to the middle of the cell. The irons fall off and the feet return.

The prisoner once again marches unhindered through the bars, passes the amazed guards and leaves the gaol. He is chased. But he runs faster than his keepers. He stops for breath round a corner, takes something from his left-hand breast pocket, bends down and unfolds it – and there is the front wheel of a bicycle! In the same way, he gets the back wheel from his right-hand breast pocket and the frame from his trouser pockets. The bicycle is assembled in an instant and he is off just as his pursuers are on the point of catching up with him.

A policeman stands in his way in the middle of the street. He stands there confidently, arms outstretched. Our thief rides directly at him and straight through him, cutting him from head to toe into two symmetrical pieces. They fall apart to left and right. Meanwhile, a billposter has arrived with ladder, paste and brush. He looks at the halves of the policeman, slaps paste onto the cut surfaces and sticks them together. The policeman comes straight back to life and rushes off after the thief.

The latter, on his bicycle, is approaching a level crossing. The gates are down and a carpenter has leant a plank against the near one. The train is approaching. Our thief rides up the plank and flies through the air, turns and, still madly pedalling, whizzes a few feet above the train through the empty air. . . .

At the beginning of the century countless such grotesque-fantastic films could be seen. Admittedly, it did not occur to any connoisseur to look for evidence of artistry in them, but they gave audiences in small cinemas precisely the fare they wanted.

The American cinema substituted for Méliès' tricks Mack Sennett's bathing beauties and the lifesavers and firemen who introduced into each film a corresponding adventure which eventually became an indispensable requisite of the comic film of the earliest period.

Méliès' romantic fantasy was transformed by the Americans' coarser delight in rough and tumble: the miraculous became the daring, the hyperbolic; the mysterious became the unexpected; romanticism became parody; and Méliès' occasionally stuffy atmosphere became slapstick comedy.

However, the line which really goes back to Méliès was not taken further after the War. In the classic period of the silent cinema[9] the fantastic film had already ceased to exist.

The cinema had become a serious bourgeois art. The slapstick of earlier years was now frowned on.

Nevertheless, the spirit of the fantastic is probably responsible for certain excursions which, in the framework of the serious film in the classic period of the silent cinema, took the form of the psychological film.

A film like *The Cabinet of Doctor Caligari* was already a long way from the 'pure foolishness' of the pre-War fantastic film. In no sense was this any longer the fairground or a popular language. However, this transplantation of the fantastic milieu into the fiction film provided a brief glimpse of what was possible, even in an ordinary film programme.

The artistic tradition within which this film unfolded was that of expressionism, a tradition that would have meant hardly anything to the frequenters of fairgrounds. Its characters are sensitive, complex, ultra-refined men and women; their sufferings, fears and dispositions are the results of an over-harsh environment.

The solution provided for the problem of Caligari – a lunatic's dream – cuts this film off completely from the world of the fantastic film of Méliès' period, unpretentious but significant in its very unpretentiousness; it cuts it off absolutely from the early grotesques, which never looked for an explanation, but simply presented the extraordinary without explanation as a miracle.

A film like Pabst's *The Secrets of a Soul*, which, setting aside its more harshly realistic means, can be described as a further development of the psychological problems introduced by *Caligari*, is even more remote from Méliès.

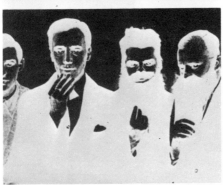

Vormittagsspuk (*Ghosts before Breakfast*). Hans Richter, 1928.

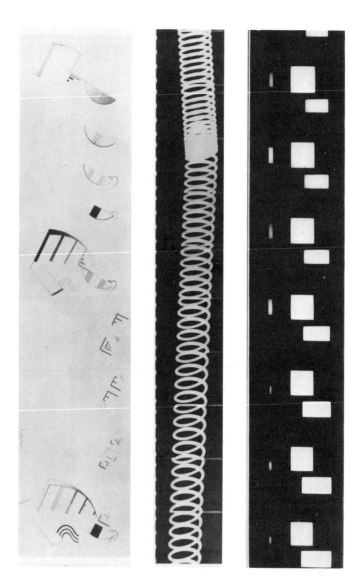

Three abstract film strips. Left to right: *Diagonal Symphony*, Eggeling;
The Return to Reason, Man Ray; *Rhythmus 21*, Hans Richter.

58

Here the clinical case is openly presented from the outset, the fantastic is made to serve the explanation of complex mental processes, without any framing device.

But while the fantastic film only survived more or less at the periphery of the fiction film, it was reinvented and rediscovered by the avant-garde cinema, which once again put the emphasis on the miraculous and the inventive enjoyed for their own sakes – René Clair's slow-motion funeral, Richter's flying hats, Disney's shooting organs.[10] Twenty years after the possibilities of the camera had been discovered, they were rediscovered by the avant-garde.

The avant-garde emerged gradually by the extension of problems posed in the fine arts: how to represent rhythmic processes not just in space and on a flat surface, but also in time. These problems led to film. Their proponents have in common the attempt to create a pure (or, as Delluc put it, 'photogenic')[11] language of cinema; to free the camera from the chains it had been in since Méliès ceased production, by the rhythm of sequences of images; to create a *film poetry* with all the means provided by the transposition of objective reality by the camera.

It is hardly surprising that the completely forgotten Méliès was repromoted by the avant-gardists and that his works won a new reputation as forerunners of theirs.

But the spirit of the avant-garde was not that of Méliès; it was the spirit of modern painting and literature. Coming from this background, the avant-gardists attempted to set cinematographic technology against the vulgar naturalistic theatricality of the fiction film. Their starting point was the presupposition that every event must first have been transformed by the camera, and that everything that had already been formed when it came before the camera should be seen only as raw material and was only significant as such. They studied the nature, properties and 'imperfections' of the camera and exploited it to the limit its construction would allow. They granted it every liberty, the actors only very limited ones. The avant-garde cinema created a new form of lyrical film.

The search for a cinematically plastic mode of expression through the freer use of the camera is not the only link between the avant-garde and Méliès: Léger's *Ballet mécanique*, René Clair's

Entr'acte, Hans Richter's *Vormittagsspuk* and *Filmstudie*, Man Ray's *Emak Bakia* and *L'Étoile de mer* represent a resurrection of both the fantastic film and the grotesque.

'The cinema must avoid any relationship
. . . with a historical, educational,
novelistic, moral or immoral,
geographical or documentary subject.
The cinema should seek to become
gradually and eventually solely
cinematic, i.e., to use only photogenic
elements.' (Jean Epstein, 1923)[12]

Historically considered, the efforts of the avant-garde represented an attempt to explode a stagnant form of the cinema, an inadequate content, a banal notion of the world we live in, to free the cinema from the strait-jacket of a tradition that was inhibiting its further development. But its experiments met little response from audiences, for elements of the grotesque had been retained and further developed within the 'official' cinema, too.

There was more than mere slapstick in Chaplin's one- and two-reelers (and often in Buster Keaton's). Without abandoning the fairground, Chaplin's and Keaton's films offered ideas and content as well as slapstick.

Chaplin and his employer, a big fat man, are pulling a cart up a hill. The cart is so heavy that they can barely manage it together. The boss is exhausted, and as he can go no further, he gets onto the cart. Little Charlie, as the servant, has thus not only to pull the heavy cart by himself, but his master as well, and the latter urges him on with a stick as if he were a donkey.[13]

Here a new element has been added to the grotesque: philosophy. Chaplin's films, even his earliest, are full of ideas which anyone can understand and yet are entertaining. The ideas never interrupt the comic plot.

This kind of cinema springs from the most primitive soil, that of the popular art of slapstick, but, without ever abandoning it, it has produced some of the finest things that have ever appeared on the screen, with what seem the simplest means. Chaplin has given

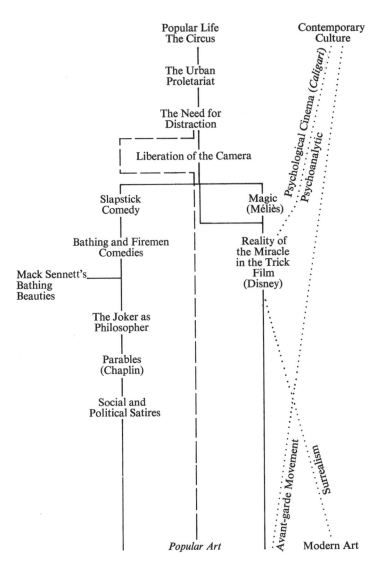

The Comic and
Fantastic Film

Popular Life
The Circus

Contemporary
Culture

The Urban
Proletariat

The Need for
Distraction

Liberation of the Camera

Psychological Cinema (*Caligari*)
Psychoanalytic

Slapstick
Comedy

Magic
(Méliès)

Bathing and Firemen
Comedies

Reality of
the Miracle
in the Trick
Film
(Disney)

Mack Sennett's
Bathing
Beauties

The Joker as
Philosopher

Parables
(Chaplin)

Social and
Political Satires

Avant-garde Movement

Surrealism

Popular Art

Modern Art

the grotesque film a philosophical content. His sufferings become an expression of the sufferings of the masses, his philosophy is theirs.

The first Chaplin films already demonstrated the mechanical style which he adapted from the circus and made his trademark.

But the outsize shoes did not remain just a crude clown's prop. With Chaplin they became the expression of a social situation, that of abject poverty. Chaplin appears as someone who cannot afford shoes that fit him. The comic effect produced by these outsize shoes, the 'shuffle' they force on him, suddenly acquired significance.

The plane of observation shifted. A crude piece of theatricality becomes a symbol. And so all the unnatural behaviour of this clown became style: in so far as a particular relation to life found artistic form.

But Chaplin's style reveals something more. It is an expression of the way one thing follows another in our lives. Like a strip cartoon, but set in motion, it suggests the implacable tick-tock of life.

This style becomes a highly significant expressive form, as if human destiny buzzed along like clockwork. This basic note becomes the melody, the rhythm of an inevitable fate.

This mechanicism is the *deus ex machina* mobilising the fantastic-grotesque life. It constitutes an essential part of the philosophy of Chaplin's style. Thanks to that style, life becomes comic, even if it is wretchedly miserable in reality, and thus acquires a symbolic perspective in the 'nonsense'. Many an abyss is revealed by this wit, it exposes injustices, social situations that have become senseless, with the result that the joke goes directly to the audience's hearts.

Chaplin has discovered and developed the principles of this mechanical method of acting. With this mechanical style, he has invented a mode of expression appropriate to the technological form of the cinema.

The Fool as Philosophical Figure

In the course of the commercial development of the cinema, the grotesque film has been displaced by the fiction film. But it has retained its own character despite the adaptation forced on it by commercial conditions. It has remained a popular art.

The fantastic film is completely humble in its origins and it has demonstrated a way of satisfying the artistic needs of the broad mass of people in a very meaningful way; not by reducing the high (traditional) arts to a lower level, but entirely out of its own resources. In the area of the fantastic film, too, there exist possibilities of contributing to the spiritual and social life of our contemporaries, of extending, enriching and enlivening their imaginations. The fool who speaks the truth is a philosophical figure. Throughout human history he has been a favourite of the lower classes, for in the roundabout manner of folly, he gives shape to their ideas, voice to their sufferings.

The potentialities of the fantastic film and the grotesque film have by no means yet been exhausted.

THE FICTION FILM

At one of the first film shows in 1895, Louis Lumière had refused to sell his patents to the enterprising young Georges Méliès on the grounds that the cinematograph was a scientific instrument rather than a machine for entertainment; the young man would only be wasting his money! Not long afterwards Monsieur Lumière had recognised the value of his invention. He and Edison were locked in a bitter struggle. Both wanted to secure the world market, for the cinema was already beginning to suggest what it was to become, an art for the masses.

It seemed destined to satisfy the universal need for entertainment and spectacle in an artistic way.

In the five centuries since the Gothic period, centuries in which the people too have been directly and actively involved in art, extraordinary things have been achieved in architecture, painting, literature, poetry, theatre and music. But these works of art

63

embody the spirit of an advanced class more than they do the general life of the people or the spirit of the lower classes of the people. The arts have become exclusive.

The cinema, on the contrary, depends on the widest possible distribution, it has to appeal to the broad masses. Here is the sole justification for its existence, and the masses, for their part, urgently require this art for the satisfaction of their aesthetic needs.

An interest in the cinema is more and more replacing interest in the other arts. Even if one regrets this on grounds of the fine arts' superior tradition, the fact can hardly be denied.

This new, vulgar art usurped some aspect of every other art, and it has a great advantage over them in the ease with which it can overcome time and space. It can take its spectators anywhere, and wherever they go they can observe everything that is going on as closely as they like. It is this capacity that makes the cinema so attractive; it satisfies the restlessness and curiosity of the age. The cinema offers the simplest form of spiritual and aesthetic 'consumption'. It is based on the most up-to-date technology, and the latter has proved a unique instrument for the development of the expression of the constantly expanding circle of modern man's ideas.

The more differentiated bourgeois art and culture became, the nearer they approached to perfection in the directions they had chosen, the clearer became the masses' demand for the cinema as an art for the masses. The enormous growth in the numbers of the lower classes and their spiritual and aesthetic rootlessness lent power to the argument and to their demand for an art corresponding to their conceptual abilities.

The cinema is a historical reaction to the perfection of bourgeois art. It develops under different conditions from those of the old arts, for its starting-point has always been the fact that it responds to, indeed is guided by, the spiritual and artistic claims of the people. Historically speaking, the cinema is an instrument for the spiritual and artistic development of the people, and the history of the art of film is not just the history of film form or the cinema industry, it is above all the history of masses in their artistic development.

Ignoring the privileged arts, technology and industry are capable of satisfying the artistic needs of the whole population. Whether a popular art can really arise on this basis, whether the product will remain dependent on social traditions, on the heritage of the older arts, on political and material interests, whether it will reflect the spirit of the people or that of the strata that make the films – these are the issues at stake in the historical struggle for the cinema, no matter how much it may seem that the audience's need for entertainment is currently satisfied in a completely 'unitary' way and the existing form of film is 'unanimously' approved.

I believe that it is easier to grasp the spirit of the contemporary cinema and to assess its developmental possibilities if one returns to the sources from which it sprang. One can only understand the current form of the cinema if one realises what difficulties had to be overcome to reach it.

However novel the problems posed by the cinema may be, it began by taking over a pre-existing tradition, that of the theatre. Its rise is unthinkable without that tradition.

The history of the fiction film as we know it today began with the introduction of actors into the cinema. This gave the cinema access to the tradition of the theatre. Here was an already existing language and conventions that the cinema could use without risk. Facial expressions and gestures that were familiar, that could express everything that one wanted to express. It was a reservoir of ideas and an artistic language with rich and well-tried means. It provided a bridge that made it easy to link the cinema with the artistic traditions of the age, and the artistic tradition of the theatre became that of the cinema.

On the roof of a tenement block one day, sets were put up and – so Henny Porten says, discussing the early days of the cinema – Messter began to film her in a (much abridged) *Das Käthchen von Heilbronn*. Smoke from the chimney pots cast a magical veil over the sets. The sun shone, Henny Porten entered stage left on cue (as was customary in the theatre), acted her scene, Messter cranked, and she exited. The whole business lasted some three to five minutes, then they were finished – as was the film. The film was the actress.

65

As representative of an artistic tradition, the actor naturally had a great influence on the development of the cinema. He knew how to express joy, sorrow, despair, happiness, life and death, and did it the way he had learnt in the theatre.

How could a story be made comprehensible on the screen? However much trouble the actor took, however clearly he tried to express himself – in this first stage of development, he could only make the most banal events comprehensible; events which were pictorially unambiguous: shooting, stabbing, fainting, weeping, raving, extreme anger, great joy. But already the connections remained unclear. What had provoked the listed emotional outbursts? Even as little as this could hardly be acted.

In order to make what was audible on the stage visible on the screen, hyper-gesticulation and hyper-expression were tried. Exaggerated gestures and mugging were used to make the connections comprehensible to the spectators even without words.

This technological deficiency, the impossibility of reproducing word and image simultaneously, gave the first impetus to the artistic development that the cinema has undergone since that time.

The style of stage acting had to be changed, the tradition of the theatre overcome. This struggle for liberation from theatrical tradition, to which the cinema owes so much, was the longest and most difficult trial that the new art had to undergo.

The first way to overcome the lack of comprehensibility attempted was the insertion of intertitles between shots. These intertitles occasionally expanded to the length of small books and thus aroused lively opposition from the audience, who had not come to the cinema to *read*.

The film actor also turned to mime for models. But mime, too, was insufficient to solve the problem of comprehensibility. To us today, these early mime films look like conversations between deaf mutes. The actor *acted* deaf and dumb, because he lacked the words which were his usual way of making himself understood.

This mime was therefore rightly supplemented by an announcer. When a girl ran on-stage (or rather, on screen) and then disappeared again, the practised tones of the commentator would be heard from the back seats: 'Well may you run, lost girl!' Or:

'Stop! stop! You are rushing to your own destruction!' And so on. For the still unskilled audiences, the announcer's explanations were often as decisive for the comprehensibility and impressiveness of the scene as the intertitles on the screen.

And if a special effort was made to add to the attractiveness of the occasional film – a historical film, say – this made it possible to tint the main characters in different colours. Thus, in a *King Lear* of 1909, when a blue girl appeared, one knew it was Cordelia; red and yellow, on the other hand, meant the bad sisters. Without such colour distinctions it would have been impossible to differentiate between the hyper-gesticulating actresses, unusual costumes and hairstyles having uniformised them, as it were.

To go with the exaggerated gestures, there were equally exaggerated facial expressions. Derivative of, but not liberated from the theatre, they became caricatures, without, however, attaining a genuine clarity in what was supposed to be being expressed.

Cinematic Space and Cinematic Time

Whereas the first stage in the development of the fiction film – say from 1895 to 1905 – was wholly dominated by imitation of the theatre, the second, lasting until about 1915, was characterised by a progressive loosening and transformation of that domination. This period saw the elaboration of a film acting style more or less the same as the one that still predominates today.

If the audience's demand for comprehensibility influenced the style of the fiction film and of the actor, forced them to change, as it were, a style of film-making came into being as a result of advances in film technology itself.

Special materials were needed for the sets, for it had been learnt that colours came out darker or lighter on film. Space was needed for light, thus restricting the actor's freedom of movement. Make-up and hairdressing had to help underline the differences between different roles and reveal their character. But what soon most sharply distinguished the cinema from the theatre was the technique of cutting and splicing on which the cinema became more and more dependent.

It was soon discovered that it was technically and economically inefficient to shoot the action in sequence and continuity. Not only did this put a technological limit on the length of a film, it also made changes of location difficult and technically complex. The film stock, which could easily be cut in two and glued together again, offered new possibilities.

And so the original reasons for the invention of the method of true editing were probably purely organisational ones. If the hero had to leave his château by the gate, the château was shot at Versailles or Sans-Souci. If the actor, having reached the terrace, was then supposed to glance over the roofs of his residence, he was shot on the roofs of Montmartre or the Friedrichstrasse, and the two shots, despite the distance between their real locations, were spliced together as spatially adjacent to one another. There thus emerged a cinematic space and a cinematic time, real space and real time were loosened and fragmented by the cinema – although at first no artistic consequences were drawn from the fact.

On the contrary: director and actor at first found the fragmentation of the ongoing action in the shooting extremely disturbing, even artistically damaging. They regarded the procedure as a necessary evil, one that clashed in particular with their image of the cinema as a means of reproducing a closed theatrical performance.

This shooting practice led to the filming of scenes only a few seconds long and then their assembly together. But as the sequence in which the scenes were shot was not that in which they made sense together, but the sequence which was most efficient for technological and economic reasons (because all the scenes took place in the same sets, or used the same actors, etc.), the real performance was interrupted. Initially, at least, to its detriment.

Whereas the actor performing scenes one after another on the stage has the chance to grow into the part and controls the modulation and climaxes of his performance himself, the film actor is entirely at the mercy of the camera technique – and eventually of the scissors during editing. The effect he can precisely calculate and immediately feel on the stage becomes quite incalculable in front of the camera. The construction of films as if with building blocks, shooting the theatrical performance bit by bit and in the wrong

68

order, finally made it necessary to discover a terser style than that of the stage actor.

For better or worse, acting technique had to adapt itself to cinematic technique: i.e., to the camera, to its optics, to the sensitivity of the film stock, the range of light available, the sets, etc.

Thus cinematic technology forced the film performer into a special kind of film acting and hence to some degree into an overcoming of the theatrical tradition.

For his part, the director was forced to find in this development methods of dramatisation that gradually separated and liberated film direction from mere imitation of the theatre.

Cinematic content, too, was drawn into the stream of this development. The ability to insert documentary elements into the fiction film, to show foreign countries and customs and to weave them into the action, and finally to make stylistic and experimental borrowings from music-hall, circus and fairground – all these things helped to loosen the dependence on the stage.

Thus if, in its first phase, the fiction film lived entirely under the aegis of imitation and the aim was still in the end entirely to give the effect of a merely reproduced theatre, in its second it was forced to acquire means of expression of a more cinematic kind.

Griffith achieved this around 1908 the moment he used cutting to separate facial expression and gestural action. He had invented the close-up.

He magnified facial expressions, the face in those moments when it has to register a movement of the soul, and thus allowed the audience a close view of internal processes and enabled the actor to convey to the audience very fine internal impulses in monstrous proportions. He then jumped back – to full figure – and the 'external' action went on.

But this method was extended to other details than just the actor's face: a giant hand that moves circumspectly to the holster and suddenly pulls out the gun – whereas a moment ago two natural-sized men had been visible – holds the spectator's attention in thrall.

In what was – by theatrical standards – the cinema's weakest point – its composite character – Griffith had discovered the element in which it was at its most effective and the starting-point for its liberation from the theatrical tradition.

His second advance after the close-up was the 'switchback'. He realised that he could remind the spectator of other scenes exactly when he wanted to by intercutting them or presenting actions taking place in separate locations alternately so that each would add to the intensity of the other. For example, he could interpolate into a series of shots showing the preparations for blowing up a bridge other shots showing a train approaching unawares, and even possibly a third group of shots showing someone desperately racing to warn the engine-driver in time.

Hence the emergence of rules for the narration of a story on film that are still valid today. The way was now open to a further development of cinematography, one essentially less bound to the theatre.

The introduction of the close-up made cinematic facial expression into a new art.

In the theatre no one had ever been able to follow the play of facial expressions to the extent that was now possible in the cinema. All the spectators can see the movements of an eyelid ten feet high, so the most delicate flutter of the heart can be expressed. This mode of expression has very little left in common with stage acting. The movement has to be performed with absolute accuracy and precision, with a complete awareness of how enormously clearly it will be visible during the projection of the film, and hence without any attempt to supplement it with bodily movement. We are no longer discussing the reproduction of a device of stage acting but rather a kind of work whose measure and meaning come only from the camera.

When Asta Nielsen lowered one corner of her mouth and pressed her lips together in a close-up, the movement was absolutely precisely calculated and the audience felt the psychological event, say, the beginnings of dislike, quite unambiguously. The less that moved in the face on the screen, the more concentrated became the spectator's attention.

But the close-up was not just a gain for facial expression. 'De Mille's film *Chicago* contains shots of the public gallery in a law court where a sensational case is being tried. There is a close-up of a bench full of girls who are following the case absorbedly with wide-open eyes, and at the same time masticating their chewing gum – their mouths working like machinery. Then comes an exciting point in the case, and again a close-up of the chewing jaws. Suddenly, as if at the word of command, they all stop chewing.'[14]

This displacement of the psychological event into a physical action, this dissection of a composite movement – this is cinematic gesture. A special kind of development begins at this point. The cinema is becoming a school for clear physical expression. It is also beginning to move away from the theatrical tradition of psychological acting, inwardly too.

Balázs cites a brilliant performance of Asta Nielsen's many years ago. 'In a certain film, she is supposed . . . to seduce a man. She feigns love and acts up with very convincing facial expressions. But in the course of the scene she really falls in love with the man. Her gestures (the same ones), her facial expressions (the same ones) gradually become sincere. She is doing just what she was doing earlier, and it is impossible to see how one can now see that she really means it.

'But there is more to come. She notices that her accomplice is watching her from behind a curtain. She must now convince him that she is only acting, just as before she was trying to convince the other man that she was sincere. The duplicity of her facial expression has turned inside out. Now, too, she is only acting, now too, what she is expressing is inauthentic. But now it is its inauthenticity that has become inauthentic. Now she is lying that she is lying.

'And all this is perceivable, without it being visible how and what she has changed in her expressions. She has invisibly taken off one mask and invisibly put on another. All this has happened "between the lines" on an invisible face.'[15]

This example does indeed express all an actress could dream of and more. But Balázs's description of it misses the crucial point. What makes it comprehensible is not the facial acting, but the way objects in the environment participate in the action: the connections that the spectator recognises: the bulge in the curtain behind which the accomplice is listening, and so on. In the right circumstances a lot more about what is exciting and dangerous in the scene, in the character's duplicity, could be revealed by the restless movements of the curtain than by Asta Nielsen's facial expressions, brilliant though they are. The same gestures would then acquire a different meaning, not just from close-ups or big close-ups and gesture and additional facial emphasis, but from the reaction of the environment.

The division of labour in the cinema between actor and object (environment) led to a change in acting style, to an integration of the actor. The latter is no longer, as in the theatre, the sole bearer of the narrative within a world of otherwise inanimate things, but, to put it crudely, no more than *one* 'thing' among others, however important.

In certain circumstances the role of principal actor may shift from a man or woman to an object. At certain moments an object can say more in the cinema than a facial expression or human action. It can say all that matters.

In a scene in Fritz Lang's *M*, one can follow the transition as the leading role shifts from actor to object. The murderer is walking with a child whom he has promised to buy a ball. The whole city is already buzzing with rumours about him, but no one knows who he is. Even in the film we have never seen his face – only his back, his hat, his shoes. The camera follows the pair, finally coming to rest on the child's hand holding the ball. A bush appears in shot and suddenly the ball rolls out from behind this bush and comes to a stop while (on the soundtrack) we hear the report of yet another child murder.

The rolling ball gives a far better idea of the child's murder than acting out the murder itself could have done.

From an object, the ball becomes a subject of the film, and arouses a greater depth of emotion than an actor could ever have done, as well as avoiding the disgust the spectator would otherwise inevitably feel.

In some twenty years' development, the cinema had evolved to the point at which it could be described without exaggeration as an autonomous art form. Materially, too, it had developed from nothing into a major industry.

The cinema had obtained international success, world-wide distribution, luxurious theatres, and the publicity that goes with them. Thanks to the excellence of its artists, it had found its place as a component part of society. It had a social function. However, this situation brought not just advantages but also restrictions. Having grown so much, the cinema was no longer free in its choice of themes, its treatment of its subject matter, its spirit, it could no longer try anything, however risky, as it had been able to when it was an insignificant medium of popular entertainment, poor in spirit and artistry. It had acquired an ever more clearly defined political and cultural mission, not just an aesthetic one, and this mission, too, had a controlling influence on its artistic development.

The artistic and social restrictions binding the cinema in its third phase – until about 1925 – were qualitatively different from those of its beginnings. If not very highly esteemed, it was at least an economically all the stronger art. The stage of experimentation was over. The costly theatres demanded more expensive films. The weight of these billions also made the cinema in some sense more respectable, more bourgeois – precisely officially 'art', too.

This completed a process of assimilation to the bourgeois arts that in some sense ran counter to the process of liberation from traditions that the cinema had earlier successfully carried out. However, some of the finest films of the silent period were being made at the same time.

Hesitantly, and in isolation from film production in the true sense and hence also from the main tasks of the cinema, the French and German avant-gardes (in reaction to the stagnation or retreat in matters of cinematic language) continued to pursue the aim of a '*pure film art*' and thus set themselves off from the tendency to reassimilate the cinema with theatre and literature.

The Russian Cinema

If the growth of the cinema in the Western world had compulsorily taken certain forms, forms dictated by the commercial positions and relative influence assigned to audience, industry, tradition and technology in the society, in the new Russia the change in the conditioning factors, the change in the relations of power and influence created a different set of preconditions for cinematic development.

As Bardèche and Brasillach's *Histoire du Cinéma* tells us, before the War, Russian cinema was distinguished from other countries' cinemas only by a certain 'melancholy' strain.[16] After the Revolution, it was a new art that had gone further along the road marked out by Griffith. While in the Western cinemas, tradition gradually re-exerted its grip, this grip was reduced in a country in which all social and political traditions had immediately been set aside by the Revolution, and in the cinematic sphere, too, the latter gave free rein to every possibility. The result was the technique of montage.

'This has up to the present been the most vigorous and stimulating move towards the emancipation of the camera,' writes Arnheim.[17] But it was not just an emancipation of the camera, it was the first true film style.

Montage consisted of a construction from extremely short fragments of scenes (montage fragments). This is appropriate to the technological structure of film, for it is 'only' the projection of many immobile individual images. The montage fragment became building material. Pudovkin went so far as to describe everything photographed as raw material and only the editing as an art form.[18] This changed the use and significance of the actor, it allowed a far more thorough-going rhythmic organisation of the series of images than had been possible hitherto. – It changed the application of the camera, it changed the spectator's position, the spectatorial plane – it changed our vision and our receptivity. It influenced not just the development of the cinema as a whole, but also that of literature and the theatre. The cinema could now attain the level of music in pictures – it could become lyrical poetry – it could even give abstract ideas a pictorial objectification.

Technically speaking, montage is only an extension of the Griffith style – for a strict division between *montage* and *cutting* is inconceivable in practice. Perhaps it would already be correct to call *montage* Griffith's double or triple scenic organisation of the attack on the railway bridge, with its three tempi, from which the Russians learnt so much.

Only at their centres are the two regions distinct, at the edges they intersect. The decisive thing about the Russians' montage technique is the direction and level of application of the cutting.

What first struck us about the Russian cinema was the astonishing number of unexpected shots. 'Montage plunged into the crowd and sought the objects for emphasis everywhere and from every viewpoint,' wrote Pudovkin.[19] At one moment the spectator found himself high over the heads of the crowd, then suddenly beneath their feet; at one moment he saw their faces, at another only their fleeing coats. It is clear that there was extraordinary freedom of choice in such a method, far more than had ever been possible in the theatre.

Griffith and his followers, too, had already abolished the 'viewpoint from the stalls' offered by the theatre, and moved the camera around. But now the spectator was plunged into the midst of the events by the camera. A hitherto unknown spectatorial plane, unattainable in any other art, had been created. On this plane the multiplicity and tempo of our lives could for the first time really be presented.

Montage has fundamentally changed filmic construction and opened up avenues that have not been exhausted even today, even if they no longer have independent significance as a stylistic form.

Among these suggestions and avenues, one of the most important is the rhythmic organisation of the film. The multitude of fragments, people, parts of people, inert objects, animals, nature, the whole animate and inanimate universe required a more thoroughly worked-out connecting organisation than had acted scenes up to one hundred feet in length. As well as the plot, the narrative, there was a need for an artistic arrangement of the short montage fragments.

Vertov, in his documentary films, was one of the first to undertake to structure the accidental rhythms of the shots, to form them artistically, and as a result he bequeathed to the cinema a musically based unity.

In the fictional montage film, this style led to the musical arrangement of pictorial expression that we admired in the furiously working machines of the fleeing Battleship Potemkin. In *The General Line*, the procession of peasants praying for rain was edited in a rhythm corresponding to the hasty – but inaudible – ringing of the bells that accompanies the procession. This gives rise to that silent cinematic music that cannot and should not be replaced by the real sound now available. – Rhythm opens up a whole new dimension to the cinema, giving it that delicate emotional effect characteristic of music. Balázs writes: 'It is unique to the rhythmic patterns of montage that elements from the most disparate spheres can be brought into counterpoint. Not, as in music, only melody with melody, not, as in architecture, only form with form. In montage, tempi and forms, movements and directions and content accents can also be tuned to one another and composed into a *single* ornamental pattern of movement. The elements thus belong to five different spheres and dimensions. Their synthesis gives rise to a sixth, something wholly new and special. A rhythmic pattern that is experienced optically and yet is invisible.'[20]

Eisenstein speaks of 'montage overtones',[21] which, like musical overtones, can only be detected by more sensitive ears, without becoming audible.

Fragmented by montage, the world was restored a unitary form by rhythm. But montage and rhythm created conditions that (at least temporarily) altered acting technique. 'For us the actor is raw material,' declared Pudovkin, 'he only acquires his true expressivity in the editing.'[22]

Thus the actor came to be inserted like a brick into a building. The direction and effect of his acting were only established by the mode of insertion. Not how and what he really acted was decisive, he only became meaningful from the context into which he was put by the pattern of the film.

For a time this outlook led to the neglect, even the exclusion of the actor: 'I prefer to take a sixty-year-old man who has had sixty years to rehearse his appearance and attitude rather than an actor who only has three days to do the same thing,' declared Eisenstein.[23] The untrained actor, the *type*, added new interest to the cinema, but the war declared on the professional actor could not, of course, be maintained, especially once the sound film had replaced the silent cinema and it was necessary to rely more and more on trained stage actors.

Culture of Optical Language

There are no authenticated reports as to how audiences reacted to the first close-ups. If they expressed astonishment, this cannot have lasted very long; they quickly got used to the many spatial and temporal 'ellipses' of film language – jumps over years, extensions of seconds – simultaneities of events in different parts of the world.

An Englishman who has travelled in central Arabia says that some Arabs could not recognise photographs taken of them. They 'recognised' nothing – for their eyes were unused to such abstractions, and they completely lacked the mediations that allow us to treat the 'abstractions' of the photograph as quite ordinary phenomena.

Balázs reckons that, ten years ago, we, too, would have been unable to understand the simplest of today's films. 'A man runs to the station after the woman he loves who is leaving. We see him rushing on to the platform. Then we see neither buildings, nor rails, nor a train. We just see a close-up of his face. Light and shade, light and shade pass alternately over the face, faster and faster. Today everyone understands: the train is just leaving.'[24]

Or: we see someone leaving a room. Then we see the room in disorder, with the signs of a struggle. Then perhaps the back of a chair from which blood is dripping. We have seen neither the struggle nor the victim – but we are in the picture. We have divined it. This montage technique of allowing things to be divined has become more and more developed, and so too has the audience's ability to follow it.

The store of optical ideas is constantly increasing. It is the presupposition for an elliptical form of expression and for a tradition on which further development can be based. The cinema's artistic technique has thus created a convention that allows us to think in an elliptical manner and even to grasp connections that we would otherwise have lacked the mental capacity to perceive. Eisenstein even describes it as the cultural mission of the cinema: 'I think the film alone is capable of making this great synthesis, of giving back to the intellectual element its vital sources, both concrete and emotional.'[25] This is precisely because it is capable of making even abstract notions concretely visible in the image.

Man is enabled, via the eye, to perceive even complex processes without difficulty. But only when the cinema had attained a certain level of development, only once it had freed itself from the crude stage of imitation, could it represent such complex processes. The latter were still unattainable for the less developed artistic form. This reveals the historical meaning of that formal development: to allow an expansion of intellectual content. This is also the form's social value.

Only in so far as the cinema freed itself from its links to the past and created its own tradition, even in the construction of the individual frame, did it become capable of capturing the great historical currents and finding an expression for them. The liberation of form (from imitation and dependence on other arts) led to a liberation of thought and vision.

The cinema has subsequently penetrated actively into the domains of all the other arts and forced them to enter into 'new combinations', to change their traditional components. The historical task that had previously fallen to the theatre was largely dissolved and taken over by the cinema. The latter then had a decisive influence on the theatre, from which, in part, it stemmed. The cinema really initiated the 'twentieth century of the other arts'. 'The cinema is the theatre's salvation,' argues Léon Sane.

Theatre, fine arts, literature were caught up in a process to which the cinema contributed. It represented the fulfilment of a wide variety of the problems of painting. It extended the visual culture achieved in painting in a direction hitherto closed to it. It taught painting how to solve the problem of movement that had, with the futurists, led to a quasi-cinematic form – and for that reason had gone as far as was possible in painting. In the abstract film the real transition from the problems of modern painting to cinema was achieved.

To literature it brought montage: the form that expresses simultaneity; to the theatre a greater spiritual freedom in dramaturgy that influenced the traditional theatrical style.

At first only an instrument for imitation and reproduction, the cinema, by liberating its form from its initial restrictions, has acquired the status of a bearer of a free spirit.

The belief in this possibility finds an expression in the optimism with which important artists have suggested that the cinema is capable of becoming the supreme artistic vision of its age.

Such a view seems justified. But in the meantime the cinema very evidently falls far short of this goal in practice.

How is it that this most modern of machines, the camera, betrays so little of contemporary reality?

How are we to explain the fact that it is not the formally unsuccessful films that tell us least about our lives, that they are not the ones least consonant with reality, that, on the contrary, it is precisely the best artists who are using the most sophisticated means to set records in the 'keeping up of appearances'?

No artistic field can be expected to produce nothing but masterpieces. But it is surely unacceptable that the most highly developed means of expression and technical equipment are generally applied to such a completely undeveloped content.

When Arnheim says that *The Student Prince* contains more art than all the 'proletarian' films ('*Arme-Leute-Filme*') put together, he may win the approval of those who want to make *Student Princes*, but such an aesthetic judgement is worthless for anyone who abominates the wax-works ideal of an absence of content clothed in a perfect form.

There is wide-ranging concern that, with a few exceptions, there are at best 'well-made' works: enthralling art, but none that is meaningful; that in all news, documentary or fiction films one can always detect the same hardly progressive spirit.

Is it not altogether unlikely that, in comparison with literature, there should be so few people with progressive ideas? Why, then, do films so lack ideas?

When expensive and sophisticated means of expression are employed, they should have some relationship to the spiritual

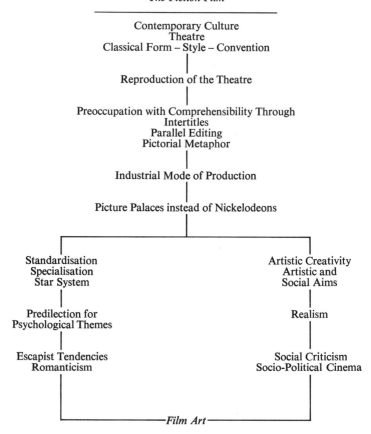

The Fiction Film

Contemporary Culture
Theatre
Classical Form – Style – Convention

Reproduction of the Theatre

Preoccupation with Comprehensibility Through
Intertitles
Parallel Editing
Pictorial Metaphor

Industrial Mode of Production

Picture Palaces instead of Nickelodeons

Standardisation
Specialisation
Star System

Predilection for
Psychological Themes

Escapist Tendencies
Romanticism

Artistic Creativity
Artistic and
Social Aims

Realism

Social Criticism
Socio-Political Cinema

Film Art

reasons for their use, they should create an image of life that justifies the deployment of such sophisticated means.

Surely the level of development of a period and of an art should be judged not just by its great achievements, but also by the achievements, great or small, that it makes impossible.

The cinema is in this nonsensical situation: on the one hand, it is one of the most interesting artistic fields of our age, a universal art, an instrument for the abolition of the opposition between thought and feeling; on the other, it is a pseudo-art with no correspondence to concrete life, an untruth constantly generating more untruth. This crass opposition reveals the contradictions to be found in the cinema, contradictions which are rooted in the age of which the cinema is a part. Our age is just as full of contradictions as the cinema, and it is the only thing that will enable us to explain this striking discrepancy.

III. [Untitled]

The progressive forces which brought about the astonishing rise of the cinema first reveal their limitations in film *content*.

In the earliest days the repertoire of the cinema consisted of a mixture of fairground, theatre and news report. As a place of entertainment with such a repertoire, the cinema was primarily aimed at a mass audience.

Only in the years immediately preceding the War did 'superior' audiences, attracted by the acting achievements of such as Asta Nielsen, Max Linder, etc., begin to get interested in the cinema.

The artistic successes of Italian, French and Swedish films especially had brought a new audience to the cinema, one which was used to going to the theatre and therefore expected not only artistic quality but also higher seat prices. The age of the Nickelodeon was over.[26]

In the meantime, cinematic entrepreneurs had managed to persuade the banks that this dubious 'industry' could also make money; they began, on credit, to build picture palaces with the plush seats appropriate to an artistically aware and concerned audience.

This audience demanded its repertoire. An art of acting that showed psychological problems and human conflicts on the screen was acceptable. With classical and historical subject matter and modern themes rearranged for the cinema, the screen was more and more monopolised by a human type with all the characteristics of a member of the 'better' classes.

Custard-pie-throwing nobodies were pushed into second place.

As at the beginning of the history of the cinema, the lower strata of the population remained the main consumers for the product, but they no longer determined the dominating spirit of film production. The latter evolved more and more towards the representation of people from the upper classes and all their characteristics, their sorrows and joys, needs and aims, their morality and their world view. All the problems of film content now revolved around them, and to an ever greater degree the cinema unearthed mental subtleties and psychological interpretations of the human type to be found in strata endowed with sufficient money and education.

It is surely no accident that, according to statistics for 1932, the theme of the struggle for social existence did not constitute one per cent of the subject matter represented in the cinema. The people we see on the embourgeoisified screen have other problems. Artistic means of expression have become more and more specialised in the cinematic portrayal of a particular class of people. What the cinema has achieved in this development is a celebration of the individual from 'better circles', of his honour and love, his conflicts, his morality, his ideals, his conceptions of social life.

Not the Western, not the documentary film, not even Chaplin and his grotesques are characteristic of the development of this branch of the cinema, which is still the dominant one today.

Having reached maturity, the cinema drew its spiritual powers from the mental world of the 'ordinary bourgeois' and, tributary to those powers, produced a number of masterpieces that can be set beside those of the theatre. The art of film having by then created an extraordinarily sophisticated armoury of expressive means, the cinema was able to surpass anything obtainable in the theatre; the result was works such as *Thérèse Raquin, Variety, The Last Laugh* and so on, consolidating the series of bourgeois films.

These films became works of art when they made real human conflicts the content of their representations, and there were directors like Feyder or Dupont who were capable of fulfilling such a prescription. Their true value lay in the ever more confident, more elliptical, more discreet and hence all the more impressive interpretation they gave of the mental life of the bourgeois individual. Hitherto the theatre had been the only place where the problems of the bourgeoisie were analysed and interpreted.

Just before the First World War, there was a very differentiated

83

bourgeois theatre of considerable psychological sophistication; this theatre had replaced the liberal or revolutionary theatre of naturalism.

The 'human individual' was the main object of literature. This individual was represented as an 'absolute', unique being, independent of society. He appeared on the stage as a doctor, an architect, a husband, a writer or a priest; as a specifically bourgeois man. It seemed self-evident that his conflicts should be treated as 'human' conflicts in general. Both literature and the theatre were preoccupied with a psychologistic mode of representation designed to reveal the principles, profundity and complexity of the conflicts of this bourgeois man. The most advanced achievements of the cinema sought to stay abreast of this development. The world revolved around the individual and not vice versa.

With this spiritual reliance on the theatre and an entrée to the cultural circles of bourgeois art, the cinema found a place in historical development and tradition.

But the cinema does not exist for the few, it is a mass art. That is its historical task.

Traditional art retains its value, it is still socially justified, even if it can only be understood and appreciated by a few – for it corresponds to a reality, a part of life.

But the cinema loses its meaning as soon as it ceases to represent spiritual 'nourishment' for the masses.

So much of most people's lives is dependent on crude material concerns that the psychologistic interpretation of the conflicts which may afflict an individual after he has satisfied his cruder material needs is quite pointless for those whose cruder material needs have precisely not yet been satisfied. Their lives provide them with no means of comparison.

The unemployed and homeless worker has mental problems, too, but they are of a different kind, because they arise on a different material basis.

This dilemma gave rise on the one hand to real works of art that extended the great tradition of the bourgeois arts in the cinema, and on the other to a false concern to make this tradition attractive to the 'people' – its vulgarisation.

84

Histoire du Cinéma remarks: 'Between the cheap films destined for the small cinemas and the super films intended for the big theatres there is really, all said and done, a difference only of more skilful production and more care for details. The inspiration in both is equally vulgar – in all but a very few exceptions.'[27]

These vulgar products, often made today with amazing technical mastery and a multitude of lifelike details, hardly have anything to do with 'bourgeois reality' any more, and nothing at all to do with that of the people.

This explains why estimations of the value of the cinema are so contradictory: on the one hand it is attributed the most universal expressive possibilities – on the other it is called a pseudo-art.

The cinema is the product of a social development that cannot be transformed or determined by artists or individuals alone. The cinema has also already grown too large and ponderous, its social ties are too strong for it to be able to leave the plane of mere entertainment all at once. But in the name of the latter the film industry rejects any possibility of offering the audience contemporary problems and demands, or new ideas, of selecting any content transgressing the bounds of approved kindergarten morality.

In this historically conditioned process we can detect the contradiction between an exclusive art and the needs of the masses of the people; it can only aggravate the problematic situation from which the cinema is suffering.

THE AUDIENCE'S WISHES

Whatever objections one may make to the industry in connection with the spiritual quality of its films, it always has one apparently irrefutable answer ready: 'The audience don't want any other kind of films but these!'

This explanation seems to confirm a certain 'psychological' diagnosis according to which the 'masses' are an amorphous entity, capable only of consumption, not of culture. No doubt such a 'recognition' does formulate the negative properties of the 'mass soul'. The evidence for it is great, and the past provides such

85

striking examples to confirm it that any belief in the spiritual development of the 'masses' must almost be regarded as utopian.

So even if the film industry wanted to propagate a different spirit from the one its products express, it would be unable to convey that spirit in its films.

The cinema audience consists overwhelmingly of the 'lower classes', of shop, office and factory workers, with their particular interests. The lives they lead are full of contradictions; the social injustices they encounter every day are not decreasing, and the outlook for change is poor.

This knowledge, conveyed to them by life itself, is not confirmed for them by the cinema in its present form. That cinema unswervingly presents a situation in which earthly and heavenly morals are complementary, in which the circumstances and opportunities of material existence are less determinant for the individual than whether he is 'good' or 'bad', i.e., whether he conforms to conventional Sunday-school morality or not. Cinematic types appear – good worker, bad employer, etc. But whether the former is 'good' or the latter 'bad' is explained only marginally by their behaviour. Rather, all these characters are to be explained by the needs imposed on them by their social situations and functions.

Nevertheless, the film audience are put on a level with school children. It is hardly surprising that such a framework allows no conflicts that correspond to the actual circumstances, and that this inhibits the free development of the cinema as an art which could take issue with life.

But how are we to explain the fact that despite this contradiction the audience still go to the cinema, indeed, apparently at least, they like films as they are?

– In the first place, by the wish to imbibe the 'moral quality' suggested by the absence of everyday cares, in the contemplation of wealth and refinement. But this attraction would surely eventually change into its opposite, into a powerful antipathy, the hitherto enjoyed 'dream fulfilment' being seen as a provocation, with revolutionary effect – yet this does not happen.

The reasons for this attitude are to be found in the special structure of human consciousness. The lower class sees the upper –

thanks to its education – as also a morally higher, better class, and attempts to imitate it accordingly. Only the upper strata are in a position, thanks to their material means, to obtain an adequate culture. This gives them a conscious superiority and the 'right' to lay down 'rules' of 'moral behaviour', of 'spiritual worth' of 'human qualities'. This 'standard' is the model for every individual striving for better conditions of existence, for everyone who wants to 'get on' in society.

Only under special historical conditions (when a society is coming apart or collapsing) are the lower strata as a whole in a position to throw off the dominant ideology. Until then they recognise it as the only valid standard; they see it as a spiritually unimpeachable value, and also as a humanly and ethically binding model, demanding imitation.

In so far as the lower strata of the population admire the wealth, modes of expression, culture and 'ideal motives' that the upper strata parade before them, this admiration, envy and yearning creates in each individual a psychological propensity to imitate the given model. Stendhal suggests that the morality of today's rulers will be the morality of their subjects in thirty years time.

In this way the 'correctness' of the ideal of social life provided by official morality is confirmed, and hence the existence of that social structure shored up.

But the film world corresponds no more to the actual life of the well off than it does to that of the office worker that secretaries regularly marry their bosses. Films are not concerned to show the reality of the upper strata, their true conflicts, to lay out their problems.

Histoire du Cinéma 'blames' Cecil B. DeMille for the invention of all those modern kitsch ingredients like sex appeal, wild parties, high-falutin' sentiments, gorgeous heroines, vamps, the rue de la Paix, and so on: 'Henceforward we were to meet with heroines dangerous enough to be alarming but still fundamentally decent enough so that all might end well. The addition of a generous share of make-believe could calm troubled consciences. . . . As the action invariably took place in high society, where, as is well known, really first-class seductions and sentiments of admirable fitness can

87

both be discovered with ease, the remoteness of the subject and the elegance of the manners succeeded in reassuring everybody at once. So it was that Park Avenue came to the screen. . . . Dazzling women, each of them gifted with extraordinary and discreetly perverse charm, now took shape on the screen against a background of the most elevating stories. . . . Cinema attitudes, cinema drawing-rooms, cinema society women, cinema sentiments, cinema adulteries and forgivenesses were established. Under the gifted, the twenty-times-creative hand of DeMille, a whole world of conventions and stupidities, destined to flourish brilliantly in the future, now took shape on the screen.'[28]

And yet another 'mass characteristic' also helped propagate such nonsense: each spectator has a set of social manners that are different from his individual manners.

A man tries to jump over a ditch and falls in. 'Oh! how out of condition I've got! Not so long ago I could have jumped over five such ditches!' He then notices that he is alone. Slowly scrabbling out of the ditch he murmurs to himself: 'You were always a weakling!'

An out-of-work journalist falls in love with a girl who turns out to to a millionaire's daughter who has run away from home. Her father has offered a ten-thousand-dollar reward for news of her whereabouts. As a result of a chain of circumstances he learns from this same out-of-work journalist (without the latter intending to tell him at all) his daughter's address. The father then takes the daughter back into the unattainable realm of millionaires and offers the young man thus cheated of his love the posted reward. The latter proudly rejects it. In the cinema the audience is, of course, collectively in favour of Clark Gable, as the out-of-work journalist in *It Happened One Night*, refusing to be corrupted, rejecting the ten thousand dollars and, morally at least, showing the mercenary millionaire 'where he gets off'; – but individually and alone almost everyone in the audience would certainly have taken the money.

However, it already requires a very subtle method of representation to induce a collective reaction of this type. If Frank Capra, the director, had not in the end brilliantly arranged for the hard-boiled millionaire to see the truth and personally help his daughter flee from the altar to where the out-of-work Clark Gable is waiting for her, the audience would probably have felt cheated of the ten thousand dollars. And rightly so! With Claudette Colbert in her lover's arms, however, this idea no longer occurs to them, and they leave the cinema in the – unjustified – belief that they, too, would have behaved just like the high-minded lover.

Nevertheless, it is not the opposite that is desirable, that, say, the journalist takes the ten thousand dollars or the secretary does not marry her boss; this would provide an acceptable solution to neither the secretary nor the journalist nor the audience. The problems would have to have been presented in such a way that the secretary and the journalist were restricted to neither of these two (impossible) solutions.

But since to pose such problems is impossible in the domain of contemporary production, which cannot discuss what is central to the mass interests of the audience, the secretary marries her boss, the journalist renounces the ten thousand dollars and the audience demands a certain attitude on the screen – even when that attitude represents a contemptuous slap in the face for them in their real situation.

The result is a life on the screen very remote from real life, a world of romanticism, an unreal, idealised representation of life without responsibilities to anything. It does not encourage comparison with reality, or even with thought at all. It only arouses unconscious feelings, memories of puberty, of the 'bitter-sweet harmony of the world', erotic daydreams apt precisely to favour a hazy, magically indistinct twilight warmth of mind and feelings.

The desire to yield to such a 'pleasure' arises from the oppressive character of daily life, not offset by any adequate spiritual and moral culture.

Rationalised working methods, the ever increasing specialisation of labour has removed from the latter the 'generally human character' it still possessed in the era of handicrafts.

Labour has lost so much of the emotional attractiveness it once had and has acquired an expressly functional character (in which the function is the obtaining of the material means of life and the

89

character that of compulsion). Free time, on the contrary, has correspondingly become emphatically non-functional – it has acquired the character of pure entertainment.

The specialised form of labour has led to a specialised form of non-labour, of 'leisure' – two spheres between which there are no longer any connections. 'To avoid catastrophe, one is forced to separate the hours of inner exaltation from daily needs. One hour of clear insight and a man would either have to kill himself or take flight into a double life,' writes Ehrenburg in his *Dream Factory*.[29]

Because this reality is no longer worth representing if one cannot at the same time show a way out of it, resort is made to the oversimplification of dreams – because the burden has become unbearable, because the contradictions of life in this transition to a new era have become more and more insoluble, there has arisen this desire for a completely unburdensome and completely thoughtless space, life on the screen has to be romanticised, there has to be love in a rose garden, women of unearthly beauty have to enjoy improbable wealth with unsurpassable passion, precisely in order that there will be not the slightest approach to reality, that no comparisons have to be made.

The Cinema as Safety Valve

The cinema fulfills this function. It is easy to understand, romantic to the point of complete anaesthesia – and compensates in a whole variety of ways for everything that is wrong with everyday life.

My explanation for the avid pleasure so many people – myself included – take in gangster films is that it is very satisfying to be able to identify with people on the screen who, armed with ingenuity, recklessness, revolvers and machine guns, can give free vent to their feelings against clearly recognisable opponents.

In this way, the individual finds a discharge for his complete impotence and fatalistic attitude to powers he has no access to.

What is wanted is to 'abreact' the burden quickly, completely and with the maximum release of nervous tension. One lives on a powder keg; in the cinema one wants to see it blow up at last.

Thus the gangster film provides a safety valve for the individual's impotent opposition.

Naturally, the spectator who is presented from stage or screen, via characters and their actions, with his own human weaknesses also has a right to demand an explanation or a solution that will help him. For if a man is shown only that he is in trouble, his interest will be minimal; but it is aroused the moment he is shown a way in which he may be able to escape his misfortunes.

There is general and justified dissatisfaction with the inconsistent treatment of subject matter. Were, say, Kleist's Michael Kohlhaas, after a hundred pages in which he has been shown to be stiff and unaccommodating, as the embodiment of obstinacy, to compromise at the end, the reader would throw the book away in disgust. The fact that Kohlhaas would rather go to the gallows than betray his person and his cause is what constitutes his greatness.

The standard solution of the happy end, on the contrary, is vulgar. For an hour and a half the protagonists 'beat the hell out of one another', but in the last few hundred feet of film they make it up.

Originally purely American, this happy end has now spread everywhere. This is very revealing as to the general level of the cinema, in which only a vulgar resolution is possible. It corresponds to the analogous crisis in a reality which makes everyday life too grey and, in compensation, has to overload the evenings with false gold. The heavier the burdens life lays on men the more they will measure up to those burdens, and the more pressing will be the demands they make of the cinema.

A VARIEGATED AUDIENCE

In another respect, too, the development of a progressive spirit in the cinema has been inhibited, and thus the producing industry has been able to avoid its moral responsibilities.

The inertia that human consciousness opposes to any innovation, however advantageous, plays a large part in all evolution. The contemporary form of cinema, too, in so far as it is influenced by its audience, is not shaped merely by their special need for entertainment, but also by their resistance to innovation, their clinging to the old.

This inertia has a different value in different historical periods. There have been many occasions in which it has been important for the maintenance of recent achievements, whereas in times of historical transformation it often represents a decelerating or even reactionary moment.

Society is just as dependent on the maintenance of what has been achieved, both spiritually and materially, as it is on progressive forces. In periods of stabilisation the traditional forces become important for the development of society. In periods of social change, of crisis, of reconstruction, on the other hand, it is the progressive drives, those setting new aims, that matter.

Whether this inertia of human consciousness is good or bad thus depends on the conjuncture, on the acute needs of society.

The stabilisation of the cinema as a particular level of vulgar entertainment, the assent of a certain part of the audience to just that form and content prove that at this stage precisely they are especially useful to that audience. There is no stage of development that does not express, for a particular part of the audience, just what it wants to cling to, what it would like to stabilise the product around.

If the circles that demand such a stabilisation of the cinema only represented a small proportion of the audience, the industry itself could validly be accused of being too spiritually inferior to give the cinema a better content.

But in reality, at this moment, a relatively large proportion of the audience approve of this 'backward' content.

The educated bourgeoisie do not reject the cinema as a kind of art, but they probably do reject the majority of the films produced, and are in principle to be counted amongst the opponents of a vulgarisation of cinematic content. Contemporary cinematic form finds hardly any support amongst them. Their culture and critical superiority – based on material security – prevent this.

But the increasing industrialisation and rationalisation of production are constantly reducing the life chances of the middle class.

Just as they struggle against their material dispossession, they fight to belong ideally to the upper classes. The less they possess, the gloomier their material prospects, the more fanatically they will cling to the trappings of their social position. To that extent they resemble Jannings in *The Last Laugh*, who risks his position as a lavatory attendant (all he has left) and steals his old hotel porter's uniform in order to be able once again – at least in appearance – to enjoy the feeling of being a 'better class of person'.

Thus the middle class build up their powers of persistence and immobility. This persistence is not just a velleity for them, they are not encouraged to this self-deception merely as a reaction to a monotonous mechanised life, rather they desperately want to believe that the out-of-work journalist really would reject the ten thousand dollars, that things really are as they are represented in the cinema, because their own inner resilience, their own mental well-being depends on it.

The task this part of the audience proposes to the film industry is to make a non-reality believable, to give it the appearance of everyday life.

The moral effect produced – as a result of the identification of the spectator with the characters in such works – is misleading and deceitful.

The oppositional forces in the audience, on the other hand, try to rebel against this because they feel, more or less clearly, that the illusions such works produce are disadvantageous to them in real life. For the spectator who has realised this, the figure of the out-of-work journalist who rejects ten thousand dollars, of the worker who rises to become a factory director, are ridiculous. And, in so far as these stories are believed by his neighbours and hence can have practical consequences – hateful. Thus for all those who reject such a falsification of life, these apparently innocuous films are revealed as *propaganda films*.

On the other hand, the audience in the cinema never respond merely passively, even if they do not applaud, whistle or laugh.

In the first place, girls have their hair cut, dress and walk like Greta Garbo or Marlene Dietrich, and young men attempt to adopt the nonchalance of Gary Cooper or Clark Gable.

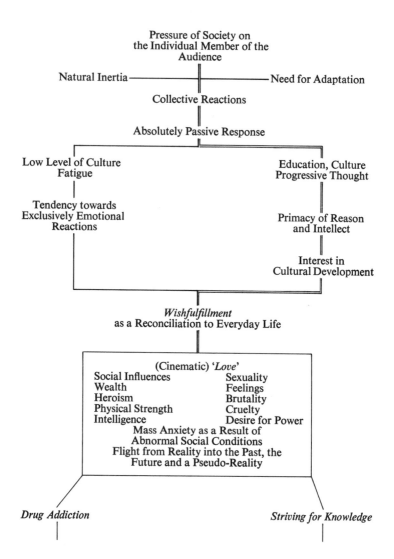

Pressure of Society on
the Individual Member of the
Audience

Natural Inertia ——————————————— Need for Adaptation

Collective Reactions

Absolutely Passive Response

Low Level of Culture
Fatigue

Education, Culture
Progressive Thought

Tendency towards
Exclusively Emotional
Reactions

Primacy of Reason
and Intellect

Interest in
Cultural Development

Wishfulfillment
as a Reconciliation to Everyday Life

(Cinematic) *'Love'*

Social Influences	Sexuality
Wealth	Feelings
Heroism	Brutality
Physical Strength	Cruelty
Intelligence	Desire for Power

Mass Anxiety as a Result of
Abnormal Social Conditions
Flight from Reality into the Past, the
Future and a Pseudo-Reality

Drug Addiction

Striving for Knowledge

Even such primitive examples show that the audience learn in the cinema and from the cinema, that they take something in – and to a certain extent also work it through.

Such an attitude is not typical of man only in the cinema. He behaves in the same way everywhere. In company, in the street, in the office, by himself – he is constantly 'working through'. If there is nothing for him to work through he is bored or becomes rebellious. But the contemporary cinema gives this eagerness for working through nothing to do.

If the audience are attacked for wanting to see nothing but *The Student Prince*, they can rightly answer that they are far too rarely given the opportunity to see anything rational.

Men do not have the same capacity for working through and learning in every period. They are only eager to learn in particular situations, e.g., when certain needs have become so pressing that they can never be stilled. At such times, progressive forces are aroused in the most obtuse. The masses then become capable of raising themselves above their average.

Unfortunately, the annals of the cinema do not give us the history of that audience which (although not the most numerous) constitutes the spirit of the audience. There are no data about the audience as promoters of development, just as there have not been enough films that have helped awaken their positive characteristics. Such a history must first be written, if we are to learn what they are capable of taking in; for hitherto there has only been a history of what they have had to put up with.

IV. Crisis

THE SOCIAL MANDATE OF THE FILM INDUSTRY

'What will happens to film depends
upon what happens to ourselves.'
(Arnheim).[30]

'Changes in the forms of the cinema, cinematic inventions, are not determined only by the creative will of the artist, rather, what the artist creates is formed under the influence of a variety of highly complex demands. These depend not just on the will of the manufacturer, however great a contribution heads of firms may make, for they are at the mercy of social pressures just as much as the artists are. Ideas grow organically in society. They are in the air looking for the hand that will catch and embody them. The will that gives rise to these ideas we call, for abbreviation's sake, the *social mandate*' (Tretyakov).[31]

Applied to the film industry this means: broadly speaking, it could not, even if it wanted to, promote a progressive line on its own; it cannot form the content as it thinks fit and create a free art if its position in society requires other things of it.

It is tied to a determinate content, the content that corresponds to its interests. It is bound to produce that content as exclusively as possible of anything else.

These are the decisive limits to the freedom of the film industry, as of any other.

Thus, as well as the more or less private aims that every individual producer pursues in his own firm, that industry represents as a whole a historical interest. Even if an individual industrialist has the humblest origins, his ownership of means of production links him indissolubly with the tendencies within his society that wish to maintain the present balance of forces, from which of course they

96

profit. Logically, they cannot and will not propagate ideas in their field that might endanger the continued existence of a situation favourable to them – even if individuals may do this, from ideal or material motives.

Unquestionably, the film industry has for many years fulfilled the mandate assigned to it by evolution – to satisfy the mass need for entertainment, instruction and art – in the most praiseworthy manner. But what was still progressive or tolerable yesterday may today be a brake on development and by tomorrow have become reactionary.

Values change to the extent that the times change.

The *social mandate* that the bourgeoisie had to carry out in the course of their rise gave us all the global concepts and views that constitute the basis of our culture. In the nineteenth century, the bourgeoisie had without question become the spiritually leading stratum of society; in a position to set aims for society as a whole.

The severe crisis in this spiritual leadership today is not so much a crisis of the ideals themselves as one of the unrealisable character of those ideals in present circumstances.

Bourgeois society has given birth to a new reality, it has opened up new possibilities through technology, the world organisation of trade and industry, possibilities that are so enormous that time is needed for society to learn to master them.

The crisis of the bourgeoisie we hear so much about is a crisis of its present form, but not one of the great ideals that have grown up along with it in the last five hundred years.

So long as social relations were still well organised, it was not difficult to carry out this social mandate. Its content was universally accepted and no one disputed it.

History is full of examples of how, under the aegis of a rising form of society, both upper and lower classes accept the symbols and forms of art with the same enthusiasm. If the continued existence of society is guaranteed, then art, too, can and must represent reality as it is – there is no need for secretaries to marry their bosses.

In periods of the rise or stabilisation of a social form, there are no signs of a *social mandate*.

97

That is why it would surely have seemed odd to describe Impressionism, with its optical ideals, its joy in nature and life, no longer needing romantic models and able to 'find beauty even in a manure heap' (Manet), as a 'social mandate'. Impressionism arose at a time when the earth was being conquered by the new technology. Nothing seemed impossible and the prospects seemed tolerable, even favourable, for the vast majority of mankind.

It is different in an era of decline, in periods of social crisis. Ideological maxims like human dignity, justice, the right to work, etc., come into such contradiction with reality (compulsion, injustice, starvation), that scepticism and disbelief erode society's underlying spiritual framework and undermine its articles of faith.

And film production is in just such a dilemma today: its interests and those of society as a whole are no longer the same.

This contradictory situation first became clearly visible in 1925 with the emergence of the Russian cinema. Antagonisms between countries resulting from the development of technology and industrial production, on the one hand, and their one-sided application, on the other, were already considerable before the War. As a result of the War, old, latent contradictions sharpened into open antagonisms.

Germany especially, the country of defeat in the War, failed revolution and rampant inflation, greeted the realistic Russian cinema as a long-awaited sign. For the first time an attempt to represent reality truthfully could be seen in the cinema. The opposition between the content of the run-of-the-mill film offerings and everyday life had been starkly revealed.

This was a turning-point in the history of the development of international film production. For the Russian cinema revealed that in films, too, one could show reality. It broke the monopoly of romantic cliché and escapist entertainment. Recognising that realism in representation and content was possible, people were made aware of the inadequacy and untruthfulness of all earlier cinema, even in its finest achievements. Conventional film content had been unmasked.

The relentless realism of the Russian films constituted the Archimedean point from which it was possible for the first time to recognise the extent of the untruthfulness and the truth-concealing methods which plagued the cinema.

The audience's reaction was almost instantaneous. Suddenly large sections of it seemed to realise that the cinema's representation of life had hitherto been a falsification. National film federations, film leagues, cine clubs, film societies, with tens of thousands of members sprang up in Germany, Holland, France, the United States and Switzerland. Thus, the screen, too, was called on to face reality.

However, for reasons already explained, the film industry could not fulfil such demands. It developed defence mechanisms corresponding to each of the stages of the struggle for the maintenance of society's existing spiritual and material aims.

The first of these stages can be characterised as a 'mediation between the opposing sides'. It corresponds to a social situation in which the contradictions have not yet grown to the point that the general public has lost its faith in the possibility of a reform and hence a reconciliation of the opposed interests.

The vast majority of French, English and American film products belong in this category. All the awkward problems thrown up by the present social situation are as far as possible avoided in order to give time for evolution to bring about a gradual reconciliation of the antagonisms.

All the more care and skill is expended in giving practically unimportant details an appearance of the utmost fidelity to nature.

When, however, in life itself – i.e., through political developments – ways and means are found for a serious alleviation of the contradictions, then the cinema is occasionally allowed a truer content.

Mister Deeds Goes to Town, for example, is a product of the policies of President Roosevelt. Such a film would have been impossible under his predecessors. These policies of social reform re-evoked an affirmative attitude, they created confidence in a juster variation of contemporary conditions.

The twenty million dollars that the tuba-playing Mr. Deeds has inherited should be given to two thousand farmers who want to work rather than fall into the hands of the villains, who already have plenty without them.

Naturally enough, this knowledge won from life itself is enthusiastically approved by the seventy-five per cent of the American people who elected Roosevelt. For he had promised them that it would be as the film suggests.

The fact that films like this are made and screened is a sign of social strength, for a change, an improvement in existing conditions can be publicly discussed.

This film and others with the same freer spirit and more life-like content came from America in the 1930s, a few also from France. They indicate the existence of healthy critical forces under existing conditions, which, in those countries, have not yet developed to the critical situation revealed by the second stage.

Films like *Mister Deeds* are, of course, allowed at certain times, but they by no means constitute the rule. In periods when conditions have become more acute, they are impossible. At such times, those films that can be described as the 'normal' ones also define the upper spiritual limit. Characteristic of this stage are a veiling and twisting of reality in the cinema. We find that rose-tinted *Student-Prince* manner I have already discussed. The cinema is following its *social mandate*: to favour and propagate an optimistic conception of existing conditions.

Plato demanded that 'education' should amount to the cultivation of perfect men. But most films would rather cultivate loyal subjects: they try to prevent the development of any other kind of perfection of the individual than the one demanded by the ruling ideology. For example, in a correct recognition of the fact that the aims of film production and those of the state lead in the same direction, the Americans many years ago made their former Postmaster General, Will Hays, the cinema's spiritual protector, giving him the job of laying down guidelines for the education of the audience by the American cinema. In this way, the industry itself created for the state an institution that directs the education of the audience along lines that co-ordinate the interests of the entrepreneurs and the state apparatus.

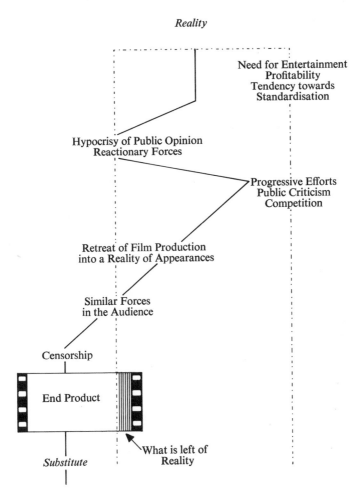

Reality

Need for Entertainment
Profitability
Tendency towards
Standardisation

Hypocrisy of Public Opinion
Reactionary Forces

Progressive Efforts
Public Criticism
Competition

Retreat of Film Production
into a Reality of Appearances

Similar Forces
in the Audience

Censorship

End Product

What is left of
Reality

Substitute

But this form of apparent self-censorship is only the most obvious form of influence. Newspaper criticism, organisations of cinema owners, private clubs (in the U.S.A., the omnipotent women's clubs) and the many other channels that help form public opinion, can encourage a quite particular taste and spirit in the cinema, and direct an unacceptable one into other channels. As a result, the spirit and taste desired by one particular side comes to look like the general one.

In those countries where the social stress is such that the antagonisms have become irresolvable, the cinema, too, is becoming more and more explicitly an instrument in a 'psychological planned economy': *propaganda*. This is the third and latest stage in the development vouchsafed the cinema. The more acute the contradictions and the broader the strata of the population adversely affected by the conditions, the more acute will become the rulers' demand that society's crucial articles of faith be defended.

During the 1930s, this 'unity' was re-established in seventeen out of the twenty-six European countries: dictatorships are in power in seventeen of those twenty-six countries.

In this context, weaknesses in the first stage of the cinema that still seemed tolerable in themselves, its shallow 'mere insignificance' and so on, take on another appearance, a *facies hippocratica*. The tendency towards romanticism, falsification, the hypertrophy of emotion, the exaggeration of sexuality, entertainment without significance, reveals itself as a symptom of decline.

Wherever the acuteness of the crisis has led to dictatorial forms of government – a proof that the antagonisms threaten to destroy the form of society – art is forced to conform to the day-to-day tactical needs of politics. In the third stage of its development, the cinema is a nationalistic cinema.

But even when the state as a national formation has become the bearer of a national culture, 'that is not part of its essence as a state, and it should not imagine that it can control culture, for it did not produce it' (Ulrich von Wilamowitz-Moellendorf).[32]

I have already demonstrated how at a certain moment the cinema began to evolve into a bourgeois art. I have referred to the conflicts that inevitably followed from this evolution. Once bound by this *social mandate* the cinema was diverted from its historical destiny (i.e., to be an art of the masses). It is therefore hardly surprising that it should have settled for a compromise form that was, in a sense, tried and tested. As we have seen, this is a compromise form that, first, is adequate to the social mandate, second – in fact only to a modest extent – maintains a certain tradition, and, third, complies sufficiently with the demands of the masses for them to acquiesce and pay.

This adaptation to the task that the cinema has been forced to carry out has led, along with a renunciation of progressive aims, to a reinforcement of commitments which are also formally retrogressive – it has strengthened the connection with the theatre.

This already recognisable evolutionary turning-point coincides with the emergence of the *sound cinema*. Naturally enough, the stagnation in the art of film has been 'blamed' on this. In reality, however, the emergence of the sound film only made the critical situation more acute, it did not actually produce it.

The limits imposed on the developmental possibilities of the cinema within the existing framework (of social contradictions) were already clearly visible in the classic silent period.

It is true that sound cinema technology produced an interruption in artistic development, because almost thirty years of experience had to be reworked. The means of expression had for the moment become much weaker and clumsier than those of the silent cinema. But if we look at the content, it is clear that there was not the slightest change. The repertoire of sound cinema content leads directly on from that of the silent cinema. The *social mandate* that had dictated the content of the silent cinema remained the same.

In a broader perspective, however, the introduction of sound made the film industry completely dependent on the electrical industry and the banks who owned the sound patents. The material risks became greater, new capital had to be invested on a large scale, and all this at a time of worsening economic crisis. The entrepreneurs had no stomach for daring experiments. They now had to be more careful than ever to adapt their films to the task of profit maximisation; for while costs were higher, linguistic barriers imposed immediate restrictions on distribution.

Thus it was not the new and unfamiliar technology that made sound films so much less mobile than silent ones, as almost all theoreticians have remarked,[33] but the absolute necessity to avoid the slightest risk.

An international film congress in Paris in 1927 investigated the limits of cinematic content. A commercial caucus pin-pointed the key task of cinematography as follows: the cinema should aim ideally to eradicate every element that imperilled the unitary character of the audience . . .!

But the more acute the antagonisms become, the more this reduction to a 'generally human' denominator reveals itself as a product of social decadence – i.e., as *wish fulfilment*.

What forms does the cinema take in the face of such facts?

What means do film producers discover to satisfy the contradictory needs of the audience, when at the same time the *social mandate* sets the narrowest limits to invention?

The instincts of the audience as consumers are investigated and tested. They are offered sugar. They are hooked on it and every encouragement is given to the mental and physical inclinations that enable them to want sugar, to swallow it and to digest it.

It is clear that such an audience has to be distinguished from one whose members are interested in the maximum development of their capabilities. The latter would have different instincts and different wishes, both physically and mentally.

Of course, it is easiest to train people to pleasure. But anyone who tolerates and encourages this cannot then claim that that is all they want, or that such a reaction is really 'generally human'.

However, the restrictions on content that this introduces and underpins have counter-effects on the form. If meaning has got to be absent, no conceivable form can create it.

While in the cinema's earliest days, it was underdeveloped forms

104

of expression and technological means that restricted the ways content could be presented, today it is the content that is inhibiting the development of the forms of expression.

'What is called Wisdom is manifested,
not in the discovery and proclamation
of Truth, but rather in the discovery of
Falsehood and in more or less refined
means of keeping it concealed. There are
some who cannot see any sign of great
masterpieces and ascribe this to the lack
of great talents. But no Homer and no
Shakespeare would be capable of putting
into verse what they want to hear.
Moreover, those people who detect no
sign of great masterpieces will manage
to get along very well without them;
though, perhaps, they could not live
with them.' (Brecht)[34]

Indeed, the representation of reality must surely be very dangerous. For the cinema goes to any lengths to encourage the evasion of awareness of it: diversion into details, into the beauties of nature, into exoticism, sexuality, the good old days, tomorrow's happiness – anything, so long as it isn't today's reality!

One can show a wealthy man who goes to Monte Carlo, gambles away all his money and then kills his wife and himself. That is a special case and not dangerous. The audience say to themselves: 'It's as unlikely that I will shoot my wife as it is that I should go to Monte Carlo.'

One can be almost pedantically realistic in the reconstruction of a certain part of the life of Henry VIII, because this king has been dead for centuries, and the conditions under which he lived have therefore acquired a legendary remoteness as far as we are concerned.

The closer a theme comes to reality, however, the more it must be romanticised and idealised. For then the other maxim comes into play, the one according to which film production influences the audience from the screen, i.e., *de te fabula narratur!*

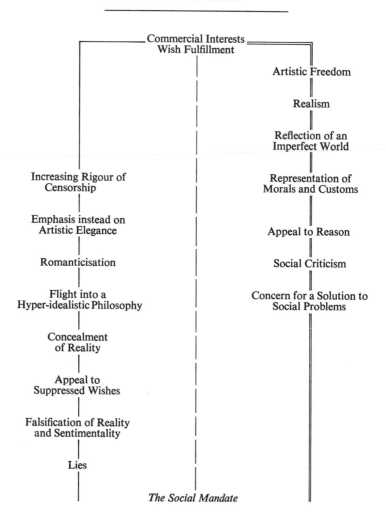

The Social Mandate

Commercial Interests
Wish Fulfillment

Artistic Freedom

Realism

Reflection of an
Imperfect World

Increasing Rigour of
Censorship

Representation of
Morals and Customs

Emphasis instead on
Artistic Elegance

Appeal to Reason

Romanticisation

Social Criticism

Flight into a
Hyper-idealistic Philosophy

Concern for a Solution to
Social Problems

Concealment
of Reality

Appeal to
Suppressed Wishes

Falsification of Reality
and Sentimentality

Lies

The Social Mandate

This is the secretary who marries her handsome boss, the out-of-work journalist who rejects ten thousand dollars. The audience, succumbing to the illusion flowing from the screen, feels 'That's my story!'

Obviously, this schematic form does not exhaust the matter. Production constantly discovers new variations, keeping always one step ahead of the receptivity of the mass of the audience. But this second category of films produces the essential 'educational' effects of the cinema, for they deal – in the suggestive form of everyday life – with the problems that the audience are involved in day in day out.

In its day an American film called *No Greater Glory* caused a sensation. It seemed to be a film of almost revolutionary pacifist content.

The children in two streets have formed gangs and are fighting for their playgrounds. At the end, one weak little boy (who, despite his lack of strength, is filled with ambition) so overdoes it that he falls ill and dies.

Such material might indeed contain a significant criticism. In the end the whole film hinges on whether the weak but heroic boy will earn the 'officer's képi' of the boys' army or not. The film is so gripping, it is made with such a refined sense of the audience's feelings, that the latter cannot but identify with the efforts of the boy, who stakes everything – his very life – on the possession of this 'officer's képi'. 'Heroically' he wins it, and 'heroically' dies doing so.

On leaving the cinema, still within its spell, one is not quite sure what the ulterior meaning is. The film is a brilliant 'mix': against war – very clearly paraded by the mother's grief; but also for the 'heroism' that stems from war; the film forces us to sympathise with the fate of its little hero in this sense. Furthermore, it is against the instinct for conquest – the fight for the playground is ridiculed; but for an education that inspires it: we share in the psychological stresses that the boys undergo in order to become victorious 'conquerors'.

And how 'lovingly' the shots, the photography have been selected for these purposes. *Knowledge* of the content never shows through. One must already *want* to know what is concealed behind it. The film is entirely directed to the *emotions*. The audience go home deeply moved; they do not really know what it is that has moved them. It was beautiful.

But what has penetrated, via their emotions, to their capacity for judgement, how they have been converted to certain views, this the audience have not noticed. It will only express itself when X and Y are discussing war. Then it will emerge that 'making war is part of human nature, and wars do inspire heroism . . .'

Could this be read in the film? All it seemed to be doing was communicating a bit of everyday wisdom – which makes it all the more dangerous.

Every film supports a particular world view. If it is our own, all right! Otherwise we must attempt, come what may, to expose the world view of that film and of other apparently even more innocuous ones. In the case of *No Greater Glory* – technically and artistically a masterpiece – most people would not accept the world view, even in the cinema they would resist it – if only they realised.

TECHNOLOGICAL PROGRESS AS AN ENEMY

When the cinema began its development, there was no technology, however revolutionary, that was not adopted straight away. Nothing was more welcome than an expansion of the technology which posed artistic problems and helped to solve new problems.

The introduction of sound technology, on the other hand, has demonstrated what material risks, losses and upheavals technology can impose on an industry whose products are highly specialised ones anyway. Patents held by non-cinematic firms act as inhibitions to development and imply the danger of a reduction in earnings.

In former times, the individual entrepreneur would have gladly welcomed sound and colour as marvellous new evolutionary forms – for his product and for his takings – and immediately applied them in his production process. Today, on the contrary, technological innovations are greeted with very mixed feelings by the film industry. There is now an antagonism between technological progress and profitability.

108

Caught in the circuit of an almost automatically advancing technology and a crisis in which the application of that very technology and of any invention that may come to advance it further can do nothing but disrupt production and cause crashes, unemployment and new crises – industry is beginning to fear technology and its constant forward drive, and to wish that a brake could be put on technology's onward movement. In a certain sense, the automatic extension of technology has become the enemy of industry which, in the present situation of damaging overproduction, does not so much want discoveries, inventions and progress as no movement at all, given that that movement may make the present situation even more difficult.

But every art has only become an art by mastering its technological means, and new technological possibilities by no means necessarily lead to the destruction of artistic development in the artistic region they affect.

For example, the discovery of perspective in the fifteenth century led to exactly the opposite, an upswing, although perspective undoubtedly forced painting into a closer imitation of nature.

In contrast to today, as we can read in the letters of Dürer, Rubens and their contemporaries, the new discovery unleashed a wave of optimism and creative enthusiasm amongst painters: precisely the enthusiasm to apply the discovery in as many ways as possible. When critics equate the closer attainment to the most exact possible reproduction of *nature* made possible by sound and colour with a decline in film *art*, this is an expression of an age that no longer has the power to sublimate its own advances and is overwhelmed by the innovations occuring every day.

Every new technological means brings us closer to naturalism, to the object, to what from an artistic viewpoint no longer needs forming – Arnheim is quite right about that.[35] But a new and different way of posing the problems is needed if we are to learn the possibilities that can be realised with a new technology – precisely what we lack today.

Hence we can only approve of a rapidly advancing technology.

Because sound, colour, 3-D lead in present conditions only to a higher degree of vulgar naturalism, their artistic prospects are

Part Two
Towards a history of the progressive cinema

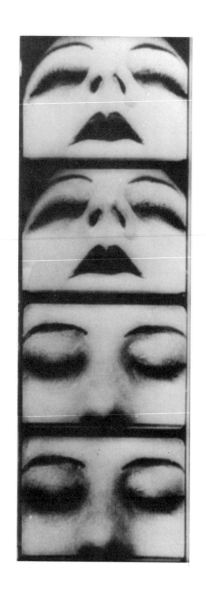

Ballet mécanique. Fernand Léger, 1924.

With a higher degree of perfection in artistic form in the cinema, a more developed artistic language and greater elegance in the achievements of direction and acting, there has also arisen a theory of film art which seeks to express the artistic value and the significance of the expressive means of each film in aesthetic principles.

There are a series of books which explain why certain achievements are particularly artistic, what constitutes their artistic value and the general principles that can be derived therefrom. These books have expounded the elements of cinematography and surveyed what has been learnt from its practical achievements.

But what is the use of a view of art that ignores or even denies the social value of the art work as a criterion? By dividing content from form, it simply sanctions the cinema's propagation of a more and more vacuous content in a more and more dazzling form.

When we are told that such and such a film is 'well made' and therefore has artistic value, while such and such another has less, because it is formally imperfect, such judgements are irrelevant – for the 'art' expended on a *Student Prince* is just as unsatisfactory to us as an audience as the inability to express a more significant content with sufficient artistry. Such an evaluation conceals what is essential.

The history of the cinema becomes incomprehensible when it is written as a history only of the official production – within which a few extravagant artists have made interesting deviations from the norm. For it is precisely in these 'extravagances' that an unusual content first finds its expression. Nothing is gained by arranging the products of contradictory world views in a single artificial line, thereby giving the impression that the cinema has developed in a spiritual and formal continuity, in one unitedly advancing complex. The habitual tendency to explain the artistic language of each artistic domain solely in its own sphere and by its own laws further reinforces the inevitable creation of an artistic space lying outside the general social space and therefore supposedly exempt from the problematic character of everyday life.

A history of the progressive cinema, however, would contain all those works that do not countenance and propagate the contemporary world as that 'best of all possible' worlds in which the secretary may marry her boss; but these are rarely whole films, often only parts or fragments which voice a different spirit from that of the official cinema.

My principal concern is to delimit the problem as a whole and to demonstrate the stages of its development. The experiment I am making here should therefore be regarded less as a history of the progressive cinema than as a hint that such a history needs to be written.

The development of the progressive spirit in the cinema does not seem to be a matter of planning. Rather it seems something unintended, and a change in social circumstances may also allow works or parts of works to appear as 'progressive' that used not to be so, either in their nature or in the intentions of their creators.

Before social development had led to the contrasts we experience today, many works we should like – retrospectively – to describe as progressive were only isolated phenomena. With the growth of the antagonisms, even the 'neutral' can come to seem partisan. The fact that forms of art, e.g., the flat roofs of houses, the brown skins of painted bodies, even a certain kind of brushwork, particular sequences of musical notes, can be described as artistically 'degenerate' shows that everything, even the tiniest details of artistic form, has become a party matter.

The struggle leads to the sharp demarcation of one kind from another. It is in this intensification of the antagonisms that lie the real origin, justification and basis for a *second* history of the cinema.

Namely: first, in the change in 'generally human' conditions and the resultant change in the social evaluation of a work of art, and, on the other hand in the force by which progress helps to determine the change in those conditions.

Second, the growing consciousness of the cinema's great historical task: from the factual representation of life via the depiction of mores, social criticism and accusation – to the consciousness of a new *social mandate* for the cinema as an art.

These factors are mutually determining. The further reactionary developmental tendencies go, the more strongly and consciously they are resisted; and the more this resistance develops an inner consciousness, the clearer will be the distinction between the two developmental lines and the more even a 'neutral' work of art will become a *prise de position*.

V. [Untitled]

The occurrence of a break with what has become standard is almost invisible. In attempting to distinguish various stages in what follows I deliberately renounce a chronological presentation. However interesting it may be to demonstrate the growth itself, dates of origins are of secondary importance in clarifying the principles and tendencies of the development, especially since all the stages were also attained side by side.

Progressive development does not proceed along a straight line, and this is true for the cinema, too. One does it most justice by describing it as a line entering and leaving the field of the official cinema in a number of different directions.

One category of these advances seems at first rather to help reinforce tendencies already present in the cinema – that group of 'extravagant' films that are concerned with the psychological problems of the individual in an unconventional, 'modern' manner.

Dreyer's *La Passion de Jeanne d'Arc* might be seen as a step in this direction. Here Dreyer is representing authentic psychological problems. His heroine suffers because she has more imagination than her fellow men, because she believes in ideas and regards their concretisation as possible and necessary. Her conflicts are those of purity and devotion and they stem from a clash with power and greed. The soul of the heroine is revealed in this collision. Psychological life as a product of the environment rather than mystically inexplicable in its origin.

To the same category belong films such as Pabst's *Secrets of a Soul* or Germaine Dulac's *La Coquille et le clergyman*. The theme itself, the representation of inner events, is perfectly neutral to start with. Emotional and psychological life has always played a

116

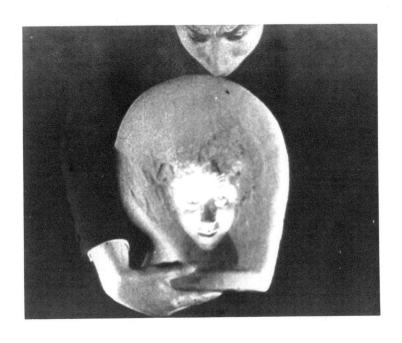

La Coquille et le clergyman. Germaine Dulac, 1927.

prominent part in the cinema. But it usually appears in a very vulgar light – for example, as if a man's happiness depended only on his inner disposition.

In fact, Pabst, Dulac and others are concerned only with the clinical phenomena of the inner life; but precisely through them they enter the field of reality and counterpose to the conventional presentation of the human interior a modern, quasi-medical one corresponding far more closely to our knowledge.

Whereas 'inner life' often appears on the screen as something inarticulate and inexpressible, Dreyer presents it as conditioned and formed by the impact of the environment, Dulac as medically analysable, and in this way the idea of the 'soul' loses some of its indefinability and mysticism.

More obviously symptomatic of the crisis in the cinema were the so-called 'proletarian' films ('Arme-Leute-Filme') that appeared in considerable numbers (and rather less considerable quality) almost everywhere in the later 1920s.

The need for reality in the cinema which the producers denied grew despite their resistance and – on a small front and for a short time – broke through the domination of convention.

This kind of production was encouraged and supported by the appearance of the Russian films. The latter demonstrated the artistic possibilities latent in a different representation of life.

But instead of following up the initial breakthrough and advancing from an inadequate formulation of the problem in terms of 'the poor' ('arme Leute') to the social theme, to the uncovering of connections, to a socially critical cinema, the makers of these films respected the conventional cinema's recipes and attempted to achieve that same sentimental and romantic impact on the audience to which the conventional cinema owes its success.

Whereas, however, romantic oversimplification is perfectly compatible with the cosmetic oversimplification of the upper-class milieu on the screen, there was a painful contradiction between that oversimplification and the brutal realism of the lower-class milieu.

The introduction of these themes presented the audience with their own reality, and they were able to verify the senselessness and untruthfulness of the proceedings on the screen against their own lives.

Not the environment, the realistic content, but a desire for more artistic form defined and sustained the third advance that took place.

With its opposition to literary imitation of the theatre and its demand for a free form of expression specific to the art of film (a 'photogenic' form of expression), the so-called avant-garde movement broke through the conventions.

As early as 1911, Canudo[36] had called for the revolutionising of the cinema by the eradication of all forms of expression that were not 'photogenic', i.e., purely cinematic, and Delluc took up the same theme. The avant-garde attacked not only the form but also the dominant spirit of the cinema as such. Unreal plots, spiritually mediocre content, lack of poetry, dependence on the theatre, one-sided privileging of the actor, all became objects of struggle.

The inhibitions imposed on the cinema by its subordination to giant organisations, material interests, distributors' tastes and political restrictions, i.e., by the constraints of its social mandate, these the avant-garde cinema broke free of in its own way. The liberation of the camera, the exploitation of all its cinematic possibilities, were put on the agenda. A social content that had lost all claim to consideràtion was replaced by a lyrico-anarchistic content apparently without any socially definable content at all.

However, this new kind of lyricism produced by the avant-garde – for example, a funeral in slow motion, a ballet of objects, games with forms, reflexes, associations between objects and living beings, dances with hats and collars, starfish and naked women's bodies – such experimental fantasies counterpose to a lyricism built into a certain bourgeois view of the world another, almost anarchistic lyricism.

This, too, however, represented a break in the dominant tradition. It, too, revealed (if only for a part of the audience) the inadequacy of the spirit conveyed by the conventional cinema and the form by which it conveyed it. It created an awareness of the need for a new form of cinema.

As soon as the cinema deals with everyday life with no intention of embellishing it, an aim becomes visible. However hesitant, any attempt to give a simple, relatively unvarnished representation of concrete life gives a glimpse of a potential new development and what it might be capable of.

A work like *Cavalcade*, a film that unfolds a piece of English history from 1870 to 1920 in epic form, in the destinies of two couples and their children, is essentially hardly any different from a conventional film, but there is one distinction. It lies not in the major artistic qualities of this film, but in the fact that it represents a concrete, not an idealised world.

The scriptwriter, Noel Coward, shows these destinies with apparent neutrality: the death of one of the sons in the upper-class family, the dissolution of strict English mores, the penetration of the servants' family into that of their masters. However, here more is at stake than the servants' daughter who wants to marry her parents' master's son, the destinies of these four old and three young people epitomise the process of a social revolution that took place in England despite the arrogance of its élite.

Thus a milieu is described and the *dramatis personae* are shifted around according to a certain moral schema, but that is not all: Coward also patiently reveals how the man is produced by the milieu, how it decisively influences him, how he belongs to it, how he himself also creates and changes it, how a life and certain mores arise within particular living conditions.

Even if Coward selects and reproduces the mores he describes without criticism, simply as facts, he marks himself off from the conventional cinema in so far as he shows individual people as products of a social development in a determinate social situation. He thus touches on connections that the conventional cinema does not even hint at.

The same is true of Flaherty. He, too, describes not people's milieux, but their mores, and in the themes he selects there is already the beginnings of a criticism.

He has almost always sought out remote regions, far from civilisation, as in *Nanook*, *Moana* and *Man of Aran*. In these regions, the struggle with nature is still the central problem, both for society and for the individual.

Flaherty's genius lies in the way he explains the life in these regions by the struggle with nature and is thus able to make his characters' behaviour comprehensible. He counterposes to the idealised world promoted by the official cinema a world in which people grow out of the conditions in which they are forced to live.

But man's struggle with nature is no longer such an important social problem for us today. Technology has relieved us of this preoccupation. Hence such themes are rather exotic for us, conquering the violence of the sea, icy cold, the tempest or wild beasts have become less significant to us than the solution of much more complex and difficult social problems.

Rotha calls this kind of documentary film idyllic documents without significance: 'It takes romanticism as its banner. It ignores social analysis.'[37]

Dinner at Eight, on the contrary, takes place in our own times and in our society.

A dinner is to take place at eight o'clock in the evening, and various different 'high society' characters have been invited to it. The failed actor, the brutal crooked businessman, his socially ambitious wife, the ruined ship-owner who is the host, his unscrupulous old flame – decline of the opulent bourgeoisie, rise of brutal crooked finance. The individual characters, their motives and their interests are presented in four parts. The fifth act that then follows depicts their meeting at dinner. The actor shoots himself, the ship-owner has to accept the financier's conditions, fates are determined and the ideals they embody are called into question.

The framework of conventional entertainment is perfectly maintained. There are criminal deals, love affairs, suspense, comedy, and this portrait of moral decadence has certainly not been painted to arouse our indignation. On the contrary, acting and direction are worldly, frivolous and cynical. But the rapid development and reconstruction of our society are capable of giving the content a more profound significance than perhaps the artist himself may have intended.

The same is also true of some of Lubitsch's films, such as *Trouble in Paradise*. In a supremely elegant way and with a cynical smile, Lubitsch presents a very refined milieu, in which the charming hero is a first-class professional thief, the manager of the lady of the house's finances an old and 'honourable' embezzler, the lady's secretary the thief's accomplice and everyone else, the lady included, a stupid or frivolous booby. Even the simplest member of the audience can see through the 'refinement' of these people and adopt a superior-critical standpoint.

And, like Lubitsch, Sacha Guitry uses comedy to reveal similar outdated notions of value as such, in order to allow the audience a productive distance.

In *Roman d'un tricheur* he 'proves', in a thoroughly worldly-wise way, that only the good do badly while the 'bad' do well; that the usual Sunday-school morality is unreal.

When the swindler tries for once to be honourable and decent, he falls again and again into the direst poverty. In the end, after a thirty-year career as an international cardsharp, he sinks to a police clerk.

Esprit français? Certainly, but the humour lies in the fact that the audience feel justified in taking the point as true to life, as an exposure of the defective morality that they have otherwise been taught to regard as sacrosanct.

Guitry does not present *the* truth here. But in contrast to the cinema's usual veiling and embellishment of life, he is at least subjectively concerned to express the truth.

The same is true of René Clair, who followed a series of satirical comedies with *Le Dernier Milliardaire*, attacking dictatorship, autarchy, militarism, money worship and servility.

A slightly crazy billionaire forces the inhabitants of a place to commit various idiocies, so they make themselves ridiculous thanks to their greed for money.

I have seen this film in a suburban cinema in Paris. The audience accompanied the 'compulsory de-individualisation' with lively interjections, leaving no doubt as to the link between this destruction of human dignity and concrete circumstances – the circumstances which had inspired the film. Their laughter was not that of

Sacha Guitry in *Le Roman d'un tricheur*, 1936.

people who have merely been tickled, it was shot through with a delight at finding their own observations confirmed, of finding themselves superior to such circumstances. Latent in this was the promise to resist them themselves should they affect their own lives.

Clair has engaged his audience from the screen in a conversation about contemporary issues and intervened in the consciousness of that audience.

If one is to believe what they say in interviews, neither René Clair not the Austro-American director and actor Von Stroheim have any other intention in their films than to express their own personal feelings and ideas; they are not concerned to exert any influence or to have any educational effect.

Stroheim, in his films, has only claimed the right to show what he thinks. In *The Wedding March* he takes a corrupt society to task, takes 'vengeance' on it, and nevertheless, the critical content is important for the ordinary cinemagoer. His individual creation acquires social significance.

And when Pabst, in *Joyless Street*, has people ruined during the inflation and queuing at the butcher's shop refused purchase of a piece of meat by the corpulent butcher that he later throws to his dog – because 'otherwise' he can't make any money out of it – then such realism strikes home in a society that tolerates such things. Pabst is not just a critic, he is an accuser.

The inescapable presupposition for an artist to be creative in our epoch, that he express a relationship to life and to the ideas of the epoch, cannot but lead him from a simple representation of reality to a *prise de position* towards it, to criticism, to accusation.

Instead of an approach that idealises human relations, the artist must be forced more and more to an unembellished representation and exposure of the social circumstances in which men are forced to act. If he does not want to lie he has no alternative but to participate in the exposure of the existing antagonisms, defects and scandals and to point out the direction in which this development is tending.

The art of film as an art of the masses was predestined to reflect the process of development of the spirit of society that we experience today. The clearer we become about the connections between the great events of the day and our own 'petty concerns', the more used we will get to following not just the destinies of individuals on the screen, but also general, supra-individual destinies – social themes. And eventually we will demand to know more about these connections that determine our fates.

It is understandable that cinematic works reflect the same social temperature scale as life. If the cinema is to get closer to social truth, it must be able to represent the whole gamut of that life. It must represent reality unvarnished, it must be able to criticise and accuse authority and argue for reason, for the right to individual freedom, for human dignity.

Viva Villa is the story of the rebellion of the cruelly oppressed people of Mexico against their tormentors. 'Viva Villa' is a battle-cry – coupled with the name of a vagabond. His story is Mexican history – so the subject is historical.

The film begins with a peon (=Mexican agricultural worker) petitioning his master for permission to get married. The bride appeals to the landowner, who owns land and people. The peon is dismissed and, when he protests, locked up. Other peons gather; they cause a disturbance and are thrown out. A few are seized, summarily tried – without any defence – condemned and hanged.

Villa, the vagabond, who in the meantime has gathered together other outlaws, arrives too late to save the prisoners. But he does find the court still in session.

The tables are turned. Villa has the hanged men cut down and seats them again in the courtroom that they left an hour earlier, still living, and 'calls on them' to pass judgement on the court or to provide grounds for the judges' innocence of their deaths. Their not unnatural silence is their hangmen's death sentence. The monstrous injustice, to our notions, whose victim one believes one is becoming, the complete destruction of individual freedom, the implacability of the compulsion create a kind of panic in the spectator so that in spontaneous indignation he demands just punishment for the inhumanity to the oppressed – and thereby individual freedom, humanity, no oppression.

So long as the screening lasts, the spectator passionately approves of proceedings he would never so unreservedly accept in his everyday life.

This phenomenon was clearest in silent Russian films which, despite their avowedly propagandistic aims, had a triumphant reception throughout the world – precisely because they attacked the problems of our epoch in an appropriate form.

An artistic masterpiece such as *Battleship Potemkin* goes so far as to abandon entirely any plot based on individual characters in favour of the representation of historical forces. *Potemkin* no longer deals with individual characters, but with masses – a ship's crew, a city.

Eisenstein is not concerned with whether the admiral who wants to have the sailors shot is personally a better or worse man than any one of the sailors. He shows the combination of historical circumstances that bring people to the point of reaction. He shows the pressure that history exerts on individuals, how 'circumstances' determine the life and actions of the individual.

Likewise in Jean Renoir's *La Grande Illusion*, in which men are shown, not in their moral attitudes, but in their reactions to the environment. The prison guard, the prisoner do not perform certain actions because they have this or that character, but out of duty, habit, compulsion, education, humanity or comradeship. This mode of characterisation by no means prevents these men from having a private psychological life, on the contrary, it is simply offered to us less indecently.

The count, the German captain, the Frenchman from the provinces, the imprisoned scholar, the Jewish businessman, all are social types as much as they are individuals.

Popular Art

Parallel to this, there has arisen from within the people themselves a different kind of *prise de position*, but one with the same historical aim. The password of this movement is *popular art* and Charlie Chaplin is its profoundest representative.

From the very beginning, Chaplin was a representative of the

Work. Chaplin, 1915.

people. In his choice of situations and types he is essentially different from the vast majority of cinema artists. In his clothes and as a type generally he has remained 'of the people'.

How much Chaplin *is* 'of the people' is proved first of all by the relation to work he brings to representation in his films.

Work at machines, in the home, on building sites, in factories is often to be seen in the cinema. Work as an activity by which people live, in so far as it is to be seen at all in the cinema, is almost always background, a setting for the action, never the action itself. Work in the cinema seems only to exist to be interrupted.

With Chaplin, precisely the reverse is the case. With a few exceptions, in which Chaplin is an idler and sets the 'elegant world' about its ears, what is at stake is always: where and how can I find work? Work, that is the great opportunity – for the out-of-work – the highest earthly happiness.

Chaplin's social plane is that of a world in which there is too little work. The action always revolves around his activity as a worker: as a prospector's assistant, as a casual worker, in the circus, as a watchmaker, as a furniture man, as an emergency help, and finally as a factory worker in *Modern Times*.

The extent to which Chaplin devotes his films to the problem of work is an expression of what is most important in his philosophy. The mixture of a passion for work (in fear of losing the job) and a tendency to sabotage that work (which often looks like a hatred for work) suggests a sense of the social worthlessness of a kind of work on which he is crucially dependent but from which in the last analysis all he gets is not to starve so long as he is able to go on working.

A second mark of the extent to which Chaplin sees the world not as top dog but as bottom dog is his attitude to eating.

Other films show us starvation: the desperate and starving unemployed of *Mister Deeds*, the hungry queues at the butcher's shop in *Joyless Street*, starvation in war films, documentaries and fiction films. In general, what is appealed to in such scenes is the spectator's pity. The proletarian Chaplin, however, has long abandoned any hope of getting something to eat by appealing to the feelings of his fellow men. Chaplin represents hunger in its practical aspect. He shows the tricks by which hunger can be stilled, or he feigns death, threatens with murder, enthusiastically presses his services, which nobody wants, speculating on gratitude and generous recompense in order to find something to eat – but he never begs.

The philosopher Chaplin shows starvation in the example of someone who recognises starvation as an inexorable fate.

There could be no greater contrast than that between the heroes of the official cinema and Chaplin. In the former we have the steadfast idler or the out-of-work journalist who rejects ten thousand dollars – in the latter a casual worker who will accept any work at all and lives at best from hand to mouth. His hunger is so authentic that extravagant gestures of nobility are completely unthinkable.

In *It Happened One Night*, Chaplin would undoubtedly have taken the money and run. But he would also share his last crust of bread with someone else who was starving.

Chaplin says that he very quickly learnt what the cinema audience wants: 'If I drop a piece of ice cream down the low-cut back of a stout, dignified woman's dress, this is, in the minds of the audience, just giving the rich what they deserve, and they delight in it. If I had dropped the ice cream, for example, on a scrubwoman's neck, instead of getting laughs, sympathy would have been aroused for the woman. Also, because a scrubwoman has no dignity to lose, that point would not have been funny. . . . People as a whole get satisfaction from seeing the rich get the worst of things, for then social justice is re-established.'[38]

Chaplin's films are full of similes. He tells his stories the way one tells stories to children, to help them understand. They seem childish and harmless.

In a very early film, Charlie arrives in a primitive society which dresses only in skins. The chief is a fat giant. All the women belong to him. Charlie, as a stranger, is welcomed with respect. He immediately adapts to the social order, and, just like the chief, knocks down the servants for no reason at all, and – when he gets the chance – knocks down the chief, too.[39]

Of course, there is no sign of open resistance or opposition to the social order in most of his films, but there are constant signs of concealed resistance. In *City Lights*, the rich playboy only recognises the down-and-out Charlie as his equal when he is drunk; when he is sober, he has him thrown out on to the street.

Modern Times no longer deals with the primitive opposition between poor and rich, elegant and shabby, which is his usual social characterisation, but with the complex role of an unemployed industrial worker who, once ejected from the production process, can no longer find any footing anywhere. Only in prison does he find respite, until such time as he will be thrown out of there, too. But now he performs his meanest action (from the prisoners' standpoint): he sides with the prison warders and betrays his escaping fellow prisoners to their truncheons. He obtains an elegantly furnished cell, with a canary in a cage. He has performed a mean action – and done very well out of it.

Chaplin has created the conventions for a language of similes in the cinema. Feeling and knowing are close bedfellows in his films, so that feeling can often be closely followed by knowledge.

The audience's understanding today is open to every kind of suggestion. The combination of censorship and an increasingly unstable reality give the audience sharper ears every day, so they often perceive more than the author himself believes he has put into his work.

In their search for confirmation for their opinions, people have such a longing for the utterances prohibited them that they think they see them even when they are not there at all. I have been told that, during the Nazi period, a big poster was put up on the advertising pillars in Berlin campaigning for some charitable cause. The poster contained a picture of a mother and child. Strangely enough, crowds gathered in front of this poster, thinking it had a hidden meaning: someone had spelt out the letters F.R.E.I.H.E.I.T. (freedom) in the drawing of the legs, shoulders arms and heads. The poster had to be withdrawn.

I have not treated Chaplin's artistic methods and his attitudes to social problems at such length because I believe he is, as it were, unique, that there are no other artists who have carried on from him in their own ways, but because he has been part of the cinema and contributed to its development from the beginning, and because he has remained the model representative of the *popular spirit* in the cinema.

The history of the progressive cinema must certainly find a place for the Marx Brothers and also Laurel and Hardy: for the Marx Brothers refuse to accept Chaplin's servile 'adaptation to life'. Rather they react with the most biting and hard-hitting satire. They show one way in which fools may speak the truth that goes far beyond Chaplin and has led them to a philosophical style of their own.

I have been concerned to note the general trend of this development, but I do not claim to have presented an exhaustive picture of it or to have represented the whole range of works. But one thing should have become clear: art – and especially film art – is called on and able to perform an important social function in this way, namely, to bring the spectators into conscious contact with reality and to put into their hands or their heads the means whereby they can recognise their real interests and act accordingly.

However, if it is the aim of the progressive cinema to intervene actively in the consciousness and emotional life of its spectators (but not to cloud their judgement), special methods have to be developed by which to carry out that aim.

Which methods are the appropriate ones for this, which ones are available or conceivable today, these questions constitute the theme and programme, the object and task of a dramaturgy of the progressive cinema.

VI [Untitled]

DRAMATURGICAL PROBLEMS OF THE
PROGRESSIVE CINEMA

The official cinema has developed a particular dramaturgy, one that suits its content, i.e., the social aims it pursues.

In the official cinema, the means have become the end – entertainment the aim itself. The audience are kept in suspense, tossed from gag to gag, until they weep, laugh, sweat and are tired out. They go home, having been 'entertained' – they are accustomed, indeed trained, to ask for nothing more.

Intercine cites a virtuoso piece of American suspense technique:

'In *Fools First* a gangster kills Raymond Griffith's brother. The body is brought by Griffith and his gang to their hideout. Knowing detectives are coming, Griffith and three other men arrange a game of poker, with the dead man's body, presumably, as one of the players.

'A fourth man, Leo White, stood behind the corpse holding the cards. When detectives arrive and try to investigate the reported slaying of Griffith's brother, Griffith forces a laugh, and points to the "obviously" living man sitting there, dealing a hand of poker. The detectives, satisfied that they have received a false report, leave.

'. . . Once the detectives have gone, Griffith goes to telephone an undertaker. Griffith merely says "One out". . . . Griffith sends for the rival gangster, gets him in the room, merches him behind a curtain, we see the curtains wave, and know that Griffith has avenged his brother's death. Griffith eventually comes to the telephone again, calls that same familiar number, and says "Make that two".'[40]

There is nothing objectionable about this method of obtaining suspense. Objections can be raised only if this method becomes the exclusive content of the film, if it is more and more skilfully and grippingly developed – but with the sole aim of so hypnotising the audience, as it were, that they are no longer capable of wanting any other content.

In fact, less 'suspense' would restore to the audience something that has been stolen from them, namely, the possibility of a more distanced and hence more critical attitude, and eighty times out of a hundred they would be capable of recognising that, except for the suspense, there is nothing worth happening on the screen. This nerve-thrilling technique has become a dramaturgical style. The presuppositions of this dramaturgical style lie partly in the technological conditions of the cinema itself. For, in the cinema, it is hardly possible technically for the spectator to have a free association with the events on the screen.

At every moment, a film may jump anywhere in space and time, and the cinema tends towards such jumps in its very technology, so the spectators must not let their concentration slip for a moment – or they may miss part of the story, part of the meaning.

Compared with music or the theatre, the cinema is dictatorial. The spectators are at its mercy, and also at the mercy of the stories that it narrates and their morality. It requires *more* strength, critical ability and will to break free of the hypnosis created by being forced to stare at the screen.

This technological characteristic is thus extremely well suited to serve the social mandate of the official cinema (to anaesthetise).

The progressive cinema, on the contrary, ought to seek a method which will enable it so to develop the audience's capacities for thought and judgement that they can link the action on the screen with their own lives, it ought to develop methods which will achieve this goal, and at the same time completely satisfy the masses' need for spectacle and entertainment. The practice of the progressive cinema, the stages in whose development I tried to trace in the last chapter, has produced different forms and methods to fulfil such a function.

For every audience, however progressive they may be, the cinema is above all a place where they expect their visual needs to be satis-

G-Men. William Keighley, 1935.

fied. Only within this framework can the questions a dramaturgy of the progressive cinema raises be concrete ones.

If the audience are insufficiently receptive – how are they to be made more so?

If they do not learn easily – how can ideas be presented in an easily accessible and forceful way?

If they only respond to primitive stimuli – how can complex contents be clothed in simple stimuli?

If they only see in their own fashion – by what means are their eyes to be opened?

If they would rather be entertained, and even badly entertained, than well taught – how can they be taught in an entertaining way?

It is hardly possible to make the audience hold their breaths more than the suspense methods of the official cinema do.

The difference between cliff-hanging gangster films such as *The Whole Town's Talking* or *G-Men* and films like *La Grande Illusion*, *Viva Villa!*, *Kameradschaft* and *Mister Deeds* . . . lies not in the quantity of the suspense, but in its quality.

The way the spectators identify is different. The same viewers who adopt an attitude of purely passive enjoyment towards a gangster film become critical, socially concerned, political judges with films such as those cited, by Stroheim, Pabst, René Clair, Eisenstein or Capra. Their ethical and spiritual capabilities are appealed to and set to work – without this 'spiritual burden' depriving them of the least part of their pleasure. On the contrary, it adds something to that pleasure, something which concerns them by no means only in the cinema.

The historical task of the progressive cinema is to develop a dramaturgy that arouses this kind of receptivity and turns people with quite primitive ideas into spectators who look for such a diet in the cinema and regard it as preferable to the other kind

The only question is, how far can one try straight away to allow spectators something more than suspense with no content; what 'devices' can be set to work to wean spectators from their addiction to the lazy diet, the uncritical identification with the performance from which they usually obtain their kicks?

In *Intercine*, Gregor describes a production of *Red Riding Hood* for children. At first the children followed the performance with great attention. The authenticity of the scenes was enthusiastically received, to the accompaniment of cheers from the audience. But when at the end the wolf 'realistically' gobbled up Red Riding Hood, the limits of reality had suddenly been transgressed, and many children left the auditorium in tears.[41]

Play, or fiction, should of course aim at illusion to the point of self-forgetfulness, but not itself become reality. If it does, opposition sets in, even fury, a fury that may be directed at the work, or, as well as the work, at its content. The cinema, with its luxurious picture-palaces, has taken this delight in illusion to extremes. Not at any price, and especially not at the price of reality, do the audience want the illusion to be broken. The fact that they reject, indeed, almost abominate, the reality that may (as it were) arise from the illusion, proves that the illusion is no simple, self-enclosed dreamed reality, but rather the audience wish to be able at the same time to maintain the latent awareness that this reality is reality, and no illusion.

Such an attitude is as characteristic of adult as it is of child audiences.

It is this 'double attitude' that enables viewers to maintain their receptivity and even their capacity for working through even as they give in to the illusion.

In fact, audiences today are more than ever prepared to *learn*, i.e., to exercise their powers of thought – if only one has managed to provide them with pleasure at the same time. It is possible to speak of a progressive activation of the audience today. The cares it brings to the steps of the cinema no longer vanish in the face of the anaesthetising screen. Man's social and hence individual position has become so insecure, so changeable today that there is a powerful moment of unrest in the contemporary spectator.

Social institutions, morality and historical concepts have come under scrutiny in so many new respects and developed in so many unexpected directions that there are no longer in principle any cinema spectators for whom these questions are not immediate vital issues.

The more the audience find reality, their everyday life, oppressive, the readier they will be to make use of their powers of thought, even at the expense of their addiction to pleasure.

DRAMATURGICAL METHODS

The official dramaturgy is concerned, in the interests of its social mandate, to represent an image of the world in which – to put it crudely – there are no other antagonisms than those between 'good' and 'bad' individuals. The moral characteristics of the individual, his dispositions and emotions, have been developed into a cliché that has long since become inadequate.

Even in *Mister Deeds Goes to Town*, this good-bad cliché is not abandoned, but carefully translated into the bad embezzling lawyers on the one hand and the simple soul of Mister Deeds on the other.

But it is misleading to tailor screen people to Sunday-school morality and thus to foster the latter by artistic means. On the contrary, it is important to know the context, because only from this knowledge is it possible to derive a genuine moral attitude. The cinema can only do this if it deals with the good and the bad, the false and the true, in a wider context than that of character, i.e., in a social context.

In an unfinished piece for theatre, the Russian writer Tretyakov has attempted to deal with what underlies the Sunday-school morality of good and bad characterisation and to analyse the socially good and bad.

The play deals with the growth of a kolkhoz from the beginning of the Revolution over more than a decade.

First Act: The peasants in the Caucasus region suffer from bandit raids. They are compelled to combine for the defence of their fields and discover amongst themselves a man of unusual courage and strategic skill. Thanks to him they are able to till their fields and just about bring in the harvest.

In this period, individuals are ranked according to their military abilities. Only the courageous are honoured – 'good' because this community needs them more than anything else.

Second Act: The bandits have been driven away for good, military abilities are no longer needed – what is, is a man with the talent for organisation, able to keep life going in the community with a few inadequate machines, a few horses and cows; – and he has to have authority over the brutalised peasants. The earlier leader retains his position in this stage, too.

But there is already friction between the warlike and the patient workers.

Third Act: In the meantime, conditions in the USSR have consolidated and machine stations are supplying whole districts with modern agricultural equipment.

The leadership of the kolkhoz now needs to contain people capable of working according to plan, considering the needs of the whole district. The leader hitherto falters. He may have been capable of making the step from warrior to leader of a brutalised band of peasants in a village whose material existence was still immediately in jeopardy, but he is no longer the right man for the third stage.

In other words, the clearer it becomes that, in this stage, the community can only flourish with the help of economic planning and organisation, the more crucial it is to get the peasants to do what is in the interests of their society by explanation and diplomacy, the less acceptable and socially beneficial becomes the leader who has hitherto received so much honour.

The ranking of 'good' and 'bad' properties has completely shifted. Almost everything that constituted a 'good' man in the first stage and, at a pinch, in the second, marks him in the third as an enemy of society: courage becomes recklessness, authority becomes arrogance, reliance on the lessons of experience becomes reaction. The 'good' man has become a 'bad' one. A peasant hardly esteemed at all so far now proves the correct leader.

It is no longer individual characters that occupy the centre of the action, but rather the development of the kolkhoz, which assigns the individual characters their importance.

Something similar happens in Eisenstein's *Potemkin*. It is not the story of a sailor that is told but one of two different social forces whose aims in life were no longer the same. However outstanding the role of the individual within this collision may have been, the social violence unleashed was no longer of a personal, individual kind.

It was Eisenstein who showed the way to a higher film form, to a modern and analytic representation of the forces of historical 'fate' – as opposed to Sunday-school morality. The success this film had throughout the world in its day proves that the mass audience are perfectly capable of following a historical argument on the screen; it proves that the 'family plot' is not a *conditio sine qua non*.

The *Potemkin* theme is obviously not a normal one but a special case; however, it shows how great the audience's interest in such a mode of treatment may be; that the cinema need not be restricted to the description of 'fates' in the narrow frame of the individual character, but can very well break out of that frame and show the social forces that underlie the individual – even if the conventional frame of the contemporary style of plot also suffers thereby.

The *unilinear plot*, as Brecht calls it, is the norm that makes the least demands on the active characteristics of the audience. Its oversimplification makes it the ideal form to avoid awakening the spectator from his sleep of illusion.

In more progressive films, it is replaced by more demanding forms. This quarrel with the conventional plot has its harbingers, though they have not always wanted quite this role. Sacha Guitry, for example, did the art of film a great service in the essayistic form he gave his *Roman d'un tricheur*. In this film, the coherent plot is broken up into a series of discussions. The ideas and life skills it demonstrates (e.g., how to deceive suspicious casino detectives) are entertaining. Guitry analyses situations: e.g., when he presents the smart location of his successful swindling activities: to the right the casino, to the left the town, to the right the palace, to the left the wretched hovels of the people. All these images are linked together by pans. This panning alone enables him to express ideas in very compressed form, as in an essay.

The grotesque, too, has never been at home with the demand for a unilinear plot. Its secondary place in cinema programmes already characterises the esteem it 'officially' enjoyed. That is why it was able to develop more independently, both in form and in content.

Hardly any of Chaplin's early shorts has a worked-out plot, but no one misses it. The framework provided by Chaplin's role – Chaplin 'as' missionary, 'as' furniture man, 'as' pawnbroker's assistant – is quite enough. *City Lights*, *The Circus*, *The Gold Rush* and *Modern Times* do have threads of action running through them, of course, but scenes are constantly interpolated which have nothing to do with the regular 'plot'. The love story with the flower girl in *City Lights* is the framework within which scenes like 'the swallowed whistle' or 'the statue of a nude woman' have no dramatic function at all. They deviate from the plot rather than carrying it forward.

The authors of *Histoire du cinéma* are only being consistent – from the standpoint of conventional production – when they regard this as an artistic failing, a result of Chaplin's relatively scriptless method; for these innumerable interruptions have nothing in themselves to do with the plot, they are only a pretext.[42]

When (in *City Lights*) a supercilious tenor is just about to sing in the rich drunkard's drawing-room and his 'refined' guests have fallen expectantly silent, this is the moment Charlie has picked to have swallowed a whistle and to be trying to cough it up. Every time he starts, the famous singer is interrupted by Charlie hiccuping and whistling, until finally he leaves the room in a rage.

This has nothing whatsoever to do with the plot. Nor does the scene in which Charlie stands in front of an art dealer's examining a bronze statue of a nude woman. Only as a 'connoisseur' of course. This prurience, so obviously concealed, generously concedes to the audience their right to their own weaknesses. These examples show – again in another respect than with *Potemkin* or Sacha Guitry – now philosophical statement is possible, precisely by more or less completely abandoning plot.

The Dramatic Film

The task of inducing not just sympathy, but also conceptual understanding and knowledge in the audience is particularly hard to fulfil in the high dramatic form. For, the greater the pathos, the more difficult it is to bring thought, too, into play.

Not for nothing did Aristotle only allow the pathetic form in epic and myth.

The less the subject matter allows contradiction, the more suited it is to the pathetic form, indeed, the more it demands it. Only what cannot be doubted may provide the content for a pathetic form. Sagas, historical subjects, the rule of fate and world history – these are the real subject matter for this style. However, knowledge of historical forces – not just mythically historical forces – makes contemporary subject matter, too, available to pathos.

In his film *Marie*, Fejös shows the sufferings a Hungarian servant girl has to undergo and the small moment of happiness she experiences before the burden of her fate (and her life) is taken from her.

Hardly any audience anywhere can fail to sympathise with this poor girl, exploited, stripped of all human rights. But this pathetically laid out material gets bogged down in lyricism. Instead of indignation, the spectator feels only a soft pity. The social consequences of the intolerable situation in which the girl lives and dies are not even hinted at in a single scene or a single figure. Fejös has neglected to raise this subject matter above the everyday and to make its 'generally human' character effective in an appropriate form, so that, in the last analysis, the achievement falls short of its subject matter.

Naturally, it is easier to impress something on someone by shocking them than by communicating the thing to them factually as a document, or satirically, ironically, parabolically, as food for thought; fear and terror are amongst the most elementary impulses to which men are subject.

That is why the pathetic form is particularly favoured when the cinema is used as an official instrument of mass influence, for the shock effects it can produce are very likely to lead to further consequences which might have been focussed in a quite different direction with a less emphatic tone.

Of all art forms, pathos is the least appropriate to provide occasion for the process of thought, to allow audiences an attitude in which they can think and not be carried away by shocks.

The Comic Film

In what form can and should an idea be expressed if free expression is obstructed or made completely impossible? One has a relatively great possibility of saying 'something' in the cinema today so long as one does so via comedy. Laughter softens censorship (whether state censorship or that of financiers, etc.) and predisposes the audience to 'swallow' all sorts of things it would violently resist if the ideas they concealed were openly presented. Laughter is the beginning of the spectator's receptivity – to the philosophical content, too.

Propaganda

In the meantime, another possibility of furthering particular aims is provided by propaganda. Propaganda today has become a science.

The economy has discovered in propaganda an indispensable aid in the sale of its products. – From simple puffing (advertisements) to hints at the social utility of its products, it has a whole range of 'methods of persuasion' at its disposal.

Thanks to the immense expansion of our technology, the possibilities of propaganda have become theoretically infinite. It has been realised that men can most easily be moulded in particular ways by approaching them *en masse*. Where consumers have to be won over, their weakest points have been sought out and methods perfected by which to strike at those weak points. It has been recognised that a product without consumers is valueless and that therefore the consumers must be co-'produced' with the commodity. As one smart advertising specialist has put it, 'Theoretically, one might even sell shoe polish as tooth paste – and vice versa.'

Propaganda has become a kind of world view, whose main dogma is that anything can be made believable. The end result is the conviction that the 'truth' is no more than a matter of better or worse propaganda, and the notion that there is in general no 'truth', that what is 'true' is just what has the power to impose itself.

Propaganda is also used by those forces who want to minimise the cinema audience's capacity for thought and knowledge. However, the English documentarist Paul Rotha arrives at the view that propaganda can also be a means for the progressive cinema – namely, so long as the ends it serves remain social ones.[43] But Rotha forgets that propaganda does not allow independent thought, it persuades by presenting pre-prepared, apparently illuminating thought models in advance of their conclusions, refus-. ing to recognise the audience's freedom of decision.

Propaganda is more and more constitutive of the content of an ideology in decline. It is an example of the alliance between reactionary forces and the film industry, against progress and for an artistic technique that serves to make the untrustworthy believable.

To make propaganda for truth, thought and judgement is one dramatic principle; propaganda for the concealment of the truth and for an uncritical reception is something else. – It is misleading to give the two the same name, for they strive for two different goals and must necessarily use different methods if they want to reach those goals.

Social Dramaturgy

It makes sense to profit by the experience of propaganda, in the art of speaking to the masses too, and hence in the cinema. But propaganda alone is too one-sided. Its only aim is to further a particular cause, whereas that of education, on the contrary, is a harmonious and meaningful formation of the whole man. It is sufficient for propaganda to hammer something in, but education aims to awaken people, stimulate them to the use of their abilities. I should like to call such a dramaturgy a 'social dramaturgy'.

In the documentary film, the main practical demand of such a social dramaturgy is to concentrate on men – not the landscape or the 'beauty' of nature. And not to 'use' those men in order to prove preconceived notions, but to observe them and to draw one's conclusions from the whole of what one sees.

The great strength of a *Nanook* or a *Man of Aran* lies in the fact that Flaherty acclimatised himself to what he wanted to present.

This enabled him to make intimate observations and to help the things he showed, the men as well as the places, to attain that language of their own which is what gives his films so much authenticity.

Ivens' tactic – '*Do not disturb!*' – should also be noted. He recommends his fellow workers to stay silently in the background, to remain as inconspicuous as possible, neither to disturb people in their work or to ask them to do the work in this way or that (because of the light, focus, or whatever). This respect shown for the object of his activity is repaid by the naturalness and the candour of that 'object'.

The fewer prejudices the documentarist brings to the solution of his task, the more easily will he be able to study the social process and the particular circumstances which have given rise to the piece of life he has to present.

Of course, a film may contain as many true details as you like, but it will remain an oversimplification unless it shows why men do the things they do. If the cinema is to communicate a knowledge of reality, it must explain the process and the necessity which have given rise to the facts shown.

The dialectical form, i.e., the form in which contradictions combine, must necessarily be the model for any representation that is to be adequate to reality. The documentarist must be capable of grasping contexts and revealing backgrounds. Only by this ability and the determination to put it into practice will he be capable of extracting a meaning from the chosen theme.

VII. Changes in the art of acting

'The theatre – despite everything – is a
moral institution, and the actor is its
curator.'

The actor is the bearer of a certain tradition. In the course of the
development of this tradition he has created certain forms and
methods of representation: what he acts influences 'how' he acts
it – and vice versa.

It is also his formative power and art that gives the theatre a
living content. By representing people on the stage he interprets
the writers' texts, filling them with meanings that change from
epoch to epoch. He interprets them according to the conceptions
that constitute the spirit of his own period, and changes in his
means of representation bring about changes in meaning.

My concern is with the way he 'resolves' contemporary people,
on stage and screen. How and by what means does he make them
come alive? How does he discipline himself and create an artistic
style appropriate specifically to the tasks of today?

Of all the artistic means on which the cinema depends, the actor
is the most strongly bound by a tradition, one that has lasted more
or less without interruption for more than two thousand years.

The cinema gained a great deal from this at first. But these
advantages soon turned out to be equally restrictions, of form and
of content. For along with the art of acting, the traditional content
and social function of the theatre were adopted in the cinema,
although the latter had quite a different social basis: the needs of
the masses. And the actor brought with him from theatre to cinema
not just a particular artistic technique, but also an equally particular interpretation of man. – The bourgeois conception of man,

with his qualities and psychological needs therefore dominated the art of acting as well. The modern actor had to produce a series of forms of psychological distinction, a series that grew steadily, in proportion to the complexity of modern problems; he had learnt to differentiate and discipline his face, his expressions to an unprecedented degree. Which explains why, at its zenith and in its greatest achievements, the style the bourgeois theatre created relied primarily on the expressiveness of its actors.

Along with such a style there grew up an audience that was prepared to follow the author and the actor and to identify intensively with such psychological interpretations.

The cinema, too, attached itself to this tradition initially and took it further, to the point of acting with a fluttering eyelid. The cinema was assigned a place alongside the bourgeois theatre.

Yet, to the extent that the bourgeois audience, too, turned to the cinema – revealing a declining interest in the theatre and its content as opposed to the cinema – the art of acting adopted by the cinema from the theatre became questionable. The actor who, for example, had developed his skill in the minute depiction of psychological states in naturalistic dramas, found only limited application and need for this ability in the cinema. The less contemporary significance the conflicts he has to represent have for us, the deeper he needs to descend into them in order to exercise his art in this way.

But if life itself destroys the value of the problems, in other words, if they become of historical interest only, their artistic interpretation also loses its value, eventually becoming no more than an aesthetic game. Then the theatre sinks into decadence. The acting is now, as Brecht puts it, only supplied and consumed in a 'culinary' way – until this 'culinary' character eventually becomes the only meaning of the performance.

Within such restrictions, the actor retains only a very minor artistic function. The fact that the only figures he has to bring to life, the only traits to which he has to lend conviction, are ones he would have very little interest in his everyday life, must be a constant frustration to him. He must become aware of the contradiction between the meaning and the practice of his activity – and hence also wish for that contradiction to be resolved.

Frank Wedekind, after a production of his *Kammersänger*, in which the ending had been changed: 'I ask myself in vain how I could have written such insipid and feeble rubbish.'[44]

There is a certain balance between actor and content that must not be disturbed. There are limits. These are overstepped whenever the charm of the acting, the kind of interpretation and the interest the audience takes in it encroach on the content. The actor can exert all his skill to make the character he is playing comprehensible. He can 'illuminate' that character even in the tiniest psychological details, without trying to make the idea the character serves comprehensible.

When an actor like Jannings as Tartuffe reveals the pathological aspect of that phenomenal hypocrite by the careful attention he pays to all his little scurrilous human features, we may, thanks to the actor's psychological profundity and empathy with his character, overlook the spiritual and moral content for which the author wrote the play. The more psychologically the details are worked out in little human touches and shadings, the weaker is our power of judgement, our receptivity for the writer's ideas. We feel what is pathological about the character represented, perhaps, instead of being above him, like the writer, and recognising his social position.

Brecht demands, on the contrary, that, where the communication of the subject matter is concerned, the spectator should not be directed into the path of empathy, there should instead be an interchange between the spectator and the actor, such that, 'basically, in spite of all the strangeness and detachment, the actor addresses himself directly to the spectator,'[45] – and hence does not lose himself completely in 'acting a man'.

Brecht said this brings the actor back to his true task: to communicate ideas to the listener.

Wedekind liked to perform the main part in his own plays. As the author, he knew best the meaning he had put in his plays and the moral effect he hoped they would have. From the start, therefore, he could strive for a certain balance between the creation

Man of Aran. Robert Flaherty, 1932–4.

148

of men on the stage and the interpretation of the ideas on behalf of which he had written the play.

His plays were no less fascinating and attractive for this division of emphasis, for the fact that one watched an elucidation of contemporary problems by theatrical means. As actor, the author had no interest in blinding his audience with fantasy. On the contrary, interpreting his own ideas, he used the dramatic form to force the spectator to take up a position in relation to the problems that interested him, and he talked to the spectator in a place that, thanks to its sacred traditions, gave his ideas an appropriate gravity.

Ferdinand Hardekopf wrote in 1911: 'The writer Wedekind himself acts the revolutionary spirits in his plays . . . and it would be an insult to him to claim that he is the greatest German actor. . . . But . . . before he takes the liberty of becoming a play-actor, he fulfils anew in each performance the masochistic duty of *play-thinking*. One would like to protest at the horrible intensity of such re-production: a fanatically suffering face conceives all the ideas of his invention once again; the central (responsible, concerned) brain struggles, in painful labour, for the *justification* of this . . . propaganda meeting.'[46]

Characteristically enough, in professional acting circles, Wedekind was regarded as a wretchedly bad actor.

In *Roman d'un tricheur*, Sacha Guitry's method is like Wedekind's. In this film, the narrative really remains a *narration*. The form of the narration allows, nay demands, an interpretation from the narrator. But if a position is taken up in relation to the events, hypnosis is interrupted by the acting. As a result, almost nowhere in the film are the spectators' powers of empathy so appealed to that he no longer realises he is a spectator. Guitry accompanies him, the spectator, ironically, cynically, entertainingly through the multitudinous ups and downs in the long life of his old rogue. He discusses the pros and cons, the moral of these experiences with the audience, as it were.

Naturally, in order to expound such a theme he needs from the audience not so much their complete identification with the characters on the screen as their realisation of the moral, social and

149

philosophical conclusions that he draws from the film scenes and of the pleasure to be got from this position of superiority.

The development of the action here very clearly becomes the (artistic) pretext for a statement about the content.

For Guitry, the actor always remains an interpreter, never becomes an auto-experiencer. He is therefore able to act his part much more 'coldly'. Conception and theme force the actor to speak as unemphatically as possible and to tune the rhythm of his movement and speech only to the need to clarify the content provided by the author.

But human representation is not excluded by this – only the hypertrophy of personality; as a result, a new relationship between the acting of ideas and the acting of people is established, a relationship in which the content regains greater significance as such.

The balance that the actor finds between the representation of men and that of ideas, the balance he evokes in the audience between the wish for surrender and enjoyment on the one hand and the pleasure of thought on the other, constitute the true guarantee that the spectator will find the work of art of practical use (in the profound sense). They also constitute the fulfilment of the social meaning of dramatic acting.

A good actor in the true sense seems to me to be simply one who recognises and fulfils these requirements. The spectator should be made capable of thinking, instead of only empathising with more or less refined psychological problems.

The contemporary cinema has produced actors who have developed an interpretative style. In *The Private Life of Henry VIII*, Laughton is at least equally the actor of a man and the clarifier of a content. He shows not Henry's psychological impulses, but his response to the environment. The subject matter is lifted out of the sphere of the purely psychological (or pathological) into a serious social perspective.

Henry VIII sits at a great banquet. Content of the scene: dining. How does a king eat? He gorges. Laughton shows that Henry VIII can permit himself to eat more vulgarly than the whole court, even the dogs. This gorging is a poetic revelation of absolute power. The actor is in no sense depicting an embarrassing character trait of a pathological individual, but rather a critical image of the social conditions.

Laughton's Henry VIII is personally neither sympathetic nor unsympathetic. He is a 'man', but not so much so that one has to identify with him completely and unconditionally. One always remains sufficiently an observer to pass judgement. That is what is good in this kind of acting; it allows us to enjoy ourselves – and also to think critically.

ADAPTATION TO THE MACHINE

Film camera and actor are mutually interdependent; they act together. This is still today a decisive problem for the cinema and for the actor especially.

According to its technological specifications, the camera can make a number of different movements whose expressive value is mechanical, i.e., produces a certain mechanical rhythm. This mechanical character is organised by the montage, by the concatenation of different sorts of movement.

The psychological actor from the theatre – what can be called the 'normal' actor – brings a certain style to the cinema based on particular rules of psychological expression. The result is a series of forms of expression (of movement) whose rhythmic organisation is psychologically determined.

Objects produced by machine act by mechanical movement and have a certain expressive character in their overall form. This expressive character is the 'form' the cinematic apparatus produces: it is the shots with their different movements, which produce together a concert of movements, an overall rhythmic expressivity.

This overall expressivity is produced by the objects on the one hand, and by the technology and its characteristics on the other. The possibility of interrupting a movement at will and combining it with another first becomes realisable as a result of the technological characteristics of the cinema, based as it is on the projection of individual frames. Depending on where I end a scene and attach it, splice it to a new one, a different emotional meaning, a different effect is produced.

151

It is therefore perfectly appropriate to speak of a certain stylistic framework prescribed for the cinema by its technology. The mechanical character of the movement of the film has its special expressivity, and artistically mastering this expressivity is as indispensable for cinematic form overall as the authenticity of the actor's performance.

In my own first naïve film experiment of 1921, *Rhythmus 21*, I tried to master the expressivity of the cinema via the organisation of the mechanical movement it contains. Vertov tried to exploit this technologically conditioned character of the cinema for artistic purposes, to plumb the artistic meaning of this technologically given necessity: *'Thought music – that is my film language!'* He exploited the 'spirit' of the technology and insisted on thinking and feeling in conformity with the apparatus, on exploiting the possibilities inherent in it. In the ordinary fiction film, it is difficult to give artistic form to the process of mechanical movement. In films as Vertov made them, scenes that had no coherence action-wise were so arranged in sequence as to bring out the formative power of their mobility. The poetic elaboration of these movements in an artistic rhythm played a decisive part not only in Vertov's films, but also in those of the early avant-garde.

As soon as the traditional actor appears, however, the problem becomes almost insoluble. Instead of an organic and artistic unity of performance and technology, there is an antagonism between the two, an antagonism between man and machine, taking three different forms which we can observe in almost every film:

– Actors' movements which are unrelated to the rhythm of the scene or the film overall;

– Shots of landscapes or immobile objects that convey the effect of sudden pauses, without being intended as such;

– movements of children, animals, objects or nature itself that arise spontaneously, their expressivity being completely unconnected with the preceding or following scenes.

In each of these three cases what can be criticised is the lack of an artistically formed expressivity of movement.

Obviously, these forms, too, have their mechanical expressivity. In such cases only plot and psychological expressivity are formed, but not the matching of both to the mechanical character of the means of expression.

Only an imperfect resolution of this contradiction can be achieved with the traditional actor, because the latter's style – mechanically uncontrollable suggestions of an inner life – represents a rhythm of its own which can be spliced into the film purely as such and as raw material, or must be wholly left out, or, as in ninety per cent of cases, reduces the film to the reproduction of an actor's performance *without* giving it an inner harmony, i.e., a rhythm.

This juxtaposition gives rise to a cinematically inadequate expressive style, even when the actor's performance is in itself outstanding.

Even a mediocre cartoon film provides more *cinematic* truth; and what is most captivating about Disney's masterpieces is their perfectly rhythmically composed and controlled movement, in image and sound.

Because the cartoon film is not capable of the completely life-like reproduction of a movement, it is forced to select. This selection (and omission) of various movements creates a mechanical style which is in ideal conformity with the technology and therefore extraordinarily effective.

For a long time – especially at the beginning of the development of the art of film – the cinema had a predilection for the representation of machines.

This predilection may be explained from the fact that, in their nature, machines are already *cinematic*, they work *mechanically*. Thanks to the precision of their movements and their succession, they produce a mechanical rhythm. Both in reality and as reproductions, machines communicate pleasure in their rhythmic 'play'.

A combination of objects which are rhythmic by nature such as machines with some acted human being will emphasise the machines and make the human being seem no more than an accessory. The machines of the fleeing battleship Potemkin, edited in a wild and precise rhythm, are maximally expressive, and certainly have no need of the support of any outlay of acting talent.

In Ivens' *Komsomol,* the people often gave way entirely to the machines, because the latter were already endowed with cinematic expressivity, while the people still lacked it on the screen.

Of all actors, Chaplin has got closest to a mode of acting corresponding to the technological character of the cinema.

From the beginning, Chaplin produced a mechanical style which enabled him to master the rhythm of his films without the mechanical character destroying the vividness of his acting. He seems to have discovered that the body is made up for the most part of levers, weights and pivots (like the camera) – and the face of muscles and surfaces that can be precisely extended and contracted. In so far as he mobilised this mechanical system in himself, he attained a harmony with the apparatus.

Chaplin's expressions and gestures were already mounted and mechanised before shooting, so his films appear to be *montage* films, without montage having been applied. They unfold according to a mechanical sequence, the individual parts of which can, as it were, be detached from one another. Feeling is not expressed as an indivisible flux, as a natural motion, but as a perfectly dismantlable and divisible process, lucidly and rhythmically organised in every gesture, in each hop, skip and jump, in the change from a smile to a blank look.

Because of this successful grasp of the technology, Chaplin abolishes the antagonism between man and machine, between art and technology, and achieves a maximum of artistic unanimity. (This seems to confirm Paul Valéry's notion that only what can be taken to pieces will work today. Or, to put it another way: we are so used to mechanical connections and mechanical operations that it is precisely, indeed only, they that are now *natural* to us.)

Chaplin's attitude is not natural in itself, but because it corresponds to the nature of the cinema, its effect is highly authentic. And he is thus able to solve the most difficult cinematic problem: to work expressions and gestures artistically into a *single* rhythm. This capacity has become his style and his films are built upon it.

But already in the early days of the cinema, an Asta Nielsen could dictate passions from the screen with the precision and economy of a machine. Laughton's acting, too, is mechanically organised. All the way through *The Private Life of Henry VIII*, he walks quite unnaturally, 'as if he had a hedgehog down his trousers'. Nobody walks like that 'in real life'. The gamut of his expressivity is reduced to different variations on immobility, as it were from one beat to the next. His facial expressions and his gestures can be dismantled, they are utilised in a crystal-clear rhythm, as with Chaplin: he makes first *one* movement, then *another*. Whether it is a matter of his face or his limbs: he *operates*.

And why is it that actors who, in other films, are mostly uninteresting, act 'well' in René Clair's films?

René Clair is one of the few masters of cinematic rhythm, one of the few who is capable of giving his films a unitary and dynamic expressivity.

In his first film, *Entr'acte*, the pattern of the movement, the change and acceleration of the rhythms, was at least as important as the literary content. A funeral with a camel drawing the hearse, filmed in slow and fast motion, works as well as it does because René Clair imbued it with the spirit of the camera. In the largos and furiosos, the andantes and adagios of the movements, he was aiming at a clear musical exp essivity. And all René Clair's films bear the same stamp. What sustains them artistically is the musicality of the movements.

FROM STAGE ACTOR TO SCREEN ACTOR

Thus two tasks in particular distinguish today's actor from yesterday's: first, he has the task of interpreting ideas, not just communicating feelings; second, he has a mechanical, not a literary-narrative function within the film.

These two tasks are interconnected. In so far as the actor represents and interprets man's concrete social behaviour – and not just an emotion – he must develop the same methods and the same economy as are also required of him by the mechanical character of the cinema, i.e., he must dismantle each expression before recapitulating it.

The screen actor has to be far more sparing than the stage actor with facial expression and gesture; first one movement, then a second, then a third; he must live and feel the rhythm of a movement as a kind of music, a melody. Only in this way can a cinematic style of acting come into being.

The same is true of dialogue: first, how is the content 'got across'? and second, how is speech integrated into the cinema's mechanical rhythm?

Not by the actor being 'natural'. The first step to be made in order to break with 'natural' acting in the contemporary sound cinema would be to speak with less identification, to express the attitude of a thinking being in the mode of speech, too. A certain coldness and hardness of tone will set bounds to empathy for the spectator and direct him more easily to what constitutes the content of the presentation.

If the dialogue is written with a feeling for the rhythmic expressivity of the words, it can only be formed artistically if it is spoken in a stylised way. One must remain at least as far from a natural mode of expression as the author of the dialogue was.

The more the actor conforms to the characteristics of the cinematic technology which is really the precondition for his own expressivity, the more that technology will support the expressivity of his acting and produce a closed form of representation. And this will be to the advantage of the content, the artistic form and the audience's receptivity, simultaneously.

If the actor is aware of the social purpose of the representation and does all he can to clarify his role in that sense, i.e., to the extent that he ceases to be a supremely sensitive actor and becomes an intelligent one, a *contemporary* one, he not only abolishes the antagonism between himself and the mechanical character of the apparatus, he also discovers in that very mechanical character his most crucial sources of assistance.

Only together with the technology, as the most modern organ of our own spirit, will the style for a contemporary content be found, too.

VIII. Relationship between word and image

Alongside the actor as presenter of human beings, the spoken word does most to form cinematic content. It can only simplify the cinema's task of telling stories. And yet the history of the cinema almost began again with the sound film.

Like the theatrical tradition, the culture of the spoken word (of the theatre) offered great advantages to the development of the cinema, for speech contributed something which could give that development a new impetus: intellectual content, the spiritual tradition of literature, the possibility of a more concentrated action.

But these advantages were bought at the cost of the inertia of that tradition and a concomitant lack of flexibility.

As a result, the spoken word was at first a highly retrogressive element. Until it had been thought through *cinematically*, had been adapted to the laws of this mechanical art, the advantages inherent in it could not be exploited, any more than the early silent cinema's reproduction of theatre had enabled it to draw immediate artistic advantages from the theatrical style.

In order to discover the significance of the word in the contemporary cinema, we must bring back the old notion of the cinema as a language of images.

Talking films are also called sound films, of course, but this designation is only technologically valid, for so long as there were no sound films it occurred to nobody to call the existing cinema the 'silent' cinema.

Sound as such would hardly have constituted an ingredient that, when added to the silent language of images, would have shattered it. Both as a rhythmic-mechanical element (music) and as natural noises sound was perfectly compatible with the framework of silent film language. There was room and an artistic function for it. Thus there were organs that could imitate the sound of falling rain, horses' hooves, roaring lions, children crying, hounds baying, birdsong, the roar of a crowd, tempests, and so on. And almost every film show was accompanied by music. Music, too, had been an active element within the framework of the silent cinema.

Meisel composed an original score for Ruttmann's *Berlin, Symphony of a City* that gave meaningful support to the life of the film, replacing the previously standard passive, ready-made form of musical accompaniment with an active one.

There were difficulties only in the ordinary acted scene. The silent cinema had such limited means that there were many things it had to ignore or else to express with a very intensive silent language of gestures. All the things we were accustomed to hearing in everyday life as noises or spoken words were translated into another, artificial world.

The language of movement was the more expressive the more actually had to be said. The mute gesture acquired importance – meaning.

In the sound cinema, on the contrary, given the concomitant language of noises and background music, the same gestures acquire an incomparably greater clarity. Even minor mistakes are obtrusive in sound film.

In early sound films, too, the dialogue was of such a low level that what mattered was not the content of what was spoken, but the mere fact that something was spoken: an exchange of 'How are you?'s was confused with dialogue.

This suggests that the problem of the sound cinema is not so much the mastering of an artistic technique as the content that the latter has been forced to serve. Only because the content is not discussed does everything seem to depend on the form.

On the other hand, on the rare occasions that there is true dialogue, it is usually clothed in a cinematic form in no way distinguishable from that of conventional 'illustration': exoticism, beauty, style, etc.

Arnheim argues that, as a means of communication discovered and used by man, speech is a part of our world, and that therefore speech should be used in the sound film primarily as a 'part of nature', as scraps of speech.[47]

Already in the early days of the sound cinema, far-reaching and imaginative experiments were made in the exploitation of the artistic possibilities of the word, of sound, of music and song.

The artistically high level of the later silent cinema, the freedom with which its means could be utilised, encouraged some people to take the same liberties with sound, too. In Ruttmann's first sound films there were astonishing acoustic montages similar to the optical ones of the silent period. The acoustic element was developed freely on the basis of the capacities of the sound camera, as yet uninfluenced by the theatre and its dialogue. King Vidor's *Hallelujah*, and other films from the very early days of sound cinema, set out to be acoustically inventive.

In Sacha Guitry's *Roman d'un tricheur*, hardly any *dialogue* is used, but instead a new form of interaction between sound and image. Speech is not used as 'nature', but in slightly rhythmical, sharply spoken punch-lines, often with an almost song-like vocal cadence.

A less naturalised use of the word, a more metrical verbalisation and pronunciation is also suggested by the mechanical nature of the cinema itself described above: the need for a rhythmic arrangement of the film's succession of movements. The spoken word, too, cannot remain outside the rhythmic life of the film. Every sound demands a general understanding for harmony, for its possibilities of combination with its neighbours, it demands flow.

For example, if one removed the rhythmic pattern, the composition, the unitary flow of the processes of mechanical movement from René Clair's films, even their raw content would become less clear, and the spiritual atmosphere which is what is so significant about such works would be very largely lost. For it is precisely his 'ballet-like' rhythm (as *Histoire du cinéma* describes René Clair's style)[48] that gives this artist's works their astonishing expressivity and overall unity. – Rhythm is no longer just a formal-aesthetic moment, it is a dramaturgical moment of the utmost importance.

The 'metrical' form of cinematic speech produced by its linking to the rhythm does not just make individual scenes more attractive, it helps to clarify the film as a whole.

Entr'acte. René Clair, 1923.

The particular form and manner one gives the rhythm, how it is conducted, depends on the dynamics of the subject matter. Every kind of subject matter has its own dynamics, defining its tempo and rhythm.

In a certain sense rhythm is a concentrating device. The expressivity of the movements is simplified in a particular (artistically felt) direction and arranged in a pattern. This pattern directs the spectator's aesthetic and musical sensibility throughout the film, and the less he notices that pattern as such, the more lasting its influence on him will be. If the rhythm stood out as such, if it triumphed as a formal element over the dynamics of the subject matter (took another direction than the one prescribed by the latter), the work would, on the other hand, be a failure – for the rhythm should be an expression of that dynamics and hence exhaustively absorbed in it.

The technique of René Clair's rhythmic style can easily be studied. However natural the steps his actors make – they are no longer natural steps, the actors caper, stagger, creep, stamp, slide or leap. No movement is so negligible that it is not organised, slightly stylised and musically felt. However delicate and elegant it is – it can often only be detected as a whole – this process is pursued absolutely consistently in every characteristic, it expounds cinematically, allowing a freer use of the word and speech.

Finally: every work of art first of all reproduces actually given things. But this power also enables it to make something dreamt apparently real, for what is dreamt is often an extension of the real. It is no accident that Méliès' early films are so concerned with magic. And, in case we have forgotten (or no longer want to admit it), there remains the invisible world, the realm of the imagination, of ideas and thoughts, a world just as real for us as the visible one. It is to find this world expressed, to feel its reality, to experience it, that we are drawn into museums, concert halls and to the magical screen.

Children as well as adults are full of this yearning for the intangible, the inconceivable, the enigmatic music of things, and this penchant for the irrational is as valuable as our pleasure in the knowledge of ideas.

The only way to make visible the otherwise invisible connections existing in the domains both of the functional and of the irrational, is still *montage*. Its struggle to embody the invisible world explains the cinema's tireless and fruitful fascination with analogies – an intensive tendency to rise to the symbolic level.

To discover the language of an exclusively pictorial formula for an inner experience, a thought, an idea, is an ambition that has almost disappeared from the cinema today, yet it probably represents the most valuable experiment in the history of cinematography, namely, to make the invisible world cinematically visible, to fuse it with the visible world into a tangible unity.

When the mobilised citizens in Trivas' *Niemandsland* first hesitantly leave their homes to report to the barracks, clutching their cardboard boxes, frightened and miserable, then, as their numbers grow, become braver, stand straighter and tread more firmly, until finally from cowards they have become ranting heroes marching in step, filled with the wish to conquer the world; this is not just a precisely realistic depiction of a walk to the barracks, but the idea of war mania itself given striking form. The coalescence of frightened individuals into wildly roaring crowds becomes the symbol of a very critical treatment of 'heroism'.

Or when, in a film such as Pudovkin's *The Mother*, the prisoner receives the message that he is to be freed, we are shown a montage of a few images: laughing children, a bubbling stream, flowering meadows – what a prisoner expects from freedom.

No one is going to take this pictorial shout to mean that children were suddenly playing, a stream bubbling, flowering meadows visible, outside the prisoner's window. Rather, the images, naturalistic in themselves, produce a conceptual idea: freedom.

The unprecedented possibilities such analogies opened up of dealing with the most profound ideas in such a way that they will be understood and remembered by the simplest intellect were presumably what once prompted Eisenstein to speak of the cinema almost prophetically as an art which, thanks to its direct visibility (a visibility that can extend even to abstract ideas), is more capable than any other of abolishing the antagonism between thought and feeling which we are so sharply aware of today.

Hence it is the machinery of the cinema, apparently so earthly, so purely physical, that has given a receptive humanity knowledge that will not be restricted to the domain of the immediate. Complex technological inventions and plans have made it possible for this machine, this refined version of the magic lantern, to make an incomparable contribution to the welfare, the recovery of humanity. If it only gets into the hands of people who are both philanthropic and ingenious, magnanimous and masters of the techniques of camera persuasion, good-natured and skilled in screen cunning.

Conclusion
Our right to the cinema

I have traced a certain development: that of the cinema as a machine for the expression of social life; and, in this context, the growth of its technological and artistic forces.

As well as representing this evolution, I have criticised it and divided the development into a progressive and a conservative, reactionary tendency. This division led, in dramaturgy, the art of acting, the composition of scenes, sets and even the construction of the individual shot, to certain demands – with the aim of inducing us, the cinema audience, to think.

Such demands neither exclude the existence of a cinema of pure entertainment (or rather: a cinema centrally concerned with the provision of entertainment), nor are they intended to interfere with our enjoyment of it. But the more sure we are of ourselves, the stronger our capacities for judgement, the more easily we can see through every type of corruption such works might produce, the less we need to be worried about consuming them.

Our delight in feminine beauty, masculine courage, our excitement at perfection, our delight in human virtues and energies will acquire a new brilliance if they are no longer used to conceal lies and stupidity.

To varnish our lives with entertaining stories is too petty a task for this mighty technology, too petty if it is to grow to artistic maturity. Let it, on the contrary, be allowed to participate in the intellectual conflicts of the age, let us dare apply this technology to shape genuine emotions, thoughts and ideas: to shape social life; it will be stimulated as never before and manage to change from a tool for more or less elegant reproduction to an instrument of genuine imagination.

Concepts such as 'human dignity' and 'freedom of thought' will characterise the history of the progressive cinema as a part of the history of the progressive spirit and of mankind in our time.

Whether freedom and progress are victorious or defeated depends on the development of which we are a part – and also on us ourselves.

May we be aware of this our responsibility.

Notes

1. Rudolf Arnheim, *Film*, trans. L. M. Sieveking and Ian F. D. Morrow (London: Faber and Faber, 1933), p. 165.
2. The film in question is *Skandal um Eva* (see film index).
3. Alberto Consiglio, 'The Spirit of the Documentary Film', *Intercine*, I (January 1935), p. 24. (*Intercine* was a multilingual journal published by the League of Nations under Arnheim's editorship.)
4. 'Der Dreigroschenprozess, ein soziologisches Experiment' in *Gesammelte Werke in 20 Bänden* (Frankfurt-am-Main: Suhrkamp Verlag, 1967), Band 18, p. 161.
5. An American series of documentary films started in 1934 under the leadership of Louis de Rochement with the aim of complementing and raising the level of the ordinary newsreels.
6. A documentary film made by Pare Lorentz in the USA in 1937 about the flooding of American rivers (see film index).
7. In 1888, Georges Méliès took over Robert Houdin's theatre of magic and illusion, added photographic slides, glass plates and projectors, and, in 1896, turned it into the first cinema.
8. Arnheim, op. cit., p. 129.
9. The years following the First World War.
10. I.e., the cartoon film *Music Land* (see film index).
11. Louis Delluc, *Cinéma et Cie, Confidences d'un spectateur* (Paris: Bernard Grasset, 1919) and *Photogénie* (Paris: Éditions de Brunoff, 1920).
12. 'De quelques conditions de la photogénie' in *Le Cinématographie vu de l'Etna* (Paris: Les Écrivains Réunis, 1926) or *Écrits sur le cinéma* (Paris: Éditions Seghers, 1974), I, p. 138.
13. *Work* (see film index).
14. Arnheim, op. cit., p. 157.
15. Béla Balázs, *Der Geist des Films* (Halle/Saale: Verlag Wilhelm Knapp, 1930), pp. 16f.
16. Maurice Bardèche and Robert Brasillach, *History of the Film*, trans. Iris Barry (London: George Allen and Unwin, 1938), p. 56.
17. Arnheim, op. cit., p. 96.
18. Vsevolod Pudovkin, *On Film Technique, Three Essays and an Address*, trans. Ivor Montagu (London: Victor Gollancz, 1929), pp. 16f.
19. Cf. ibid., pp. 145ff.
20. Balázs, op. cit., pp. 6of.

21. Cit. Balázs, op. cit., p. 61.
22. Cf. Pudovkin, op. cit., pp. 18f., 130ff. and 134.
23. Richter's own record of a conversation with Eisenstein.
24. Balázs, op. cit., pp. 3ff.
25. At a lecture in Paris, 17 February, 1930, cit. Balázs, op. cit., p. 89 and Bardèche and Brasillach, op. cit., p. 273.
26. The first cinemas in America were adapted shops with an admission price of five cents or a nickel, hence the name 'nickelodeon'.
27. Bardèche and Brasillach, op. cit., p. 373.
28. Ibid., pp. 203f.
29. Ilya Ehrenburg, *Die Traumfabrik, Chronik des Films* (Berlin: Malik-Verlag, 1931). The passage quoted is not to be found in the German or French editions.
30. Arnheim, op. cit., p. 296.
31. Personal communication from Tretyakov to Richter. Cf. also Sergei Tretyakov, 'Unser Kino' in *Die Arbeit des Schriftstellers, Aufsätze Reportagen Porträts* (Reineck bei Hamburg: Rowohlt, 1972), pp. 57–73.
32. 'Volk, Staat, Sprache', speech of 27 January, 1898, in *Reden und Vorträge*, 3rd ed. (Berlin: Weidmannsche Buchhandlung, 1913), p. 148.
33. Richter is here referring to Arnheim and Balázs.
34. *The Mother, with Notes by Bertolt Brecht*, trans. Lee Baxandall (New York: Grove Press, 1965), p. 156.
35. Arnheim, op. cit., pp. 283ff.
36. Ricciotto Canudo, 'Il Manifesto delle sette arte' (1911) in *L'Usine aux images* (Geneva: Office Central, 1927).
37. Paul Rotha, *Documentary Film* (London: Faber and Faber, 1936), p. 120.
38. Charlie Chaplin, 'What People Laugh At', *The American Magazine*, LXXXVI, 5 (November 1918), pp. 34 and 134. Richter, or his German source, offers a paraphrase of Chaplin's words. The last sentence, in particular, originally reads: 'The reason for this, of course, lies in the fact that nine tenths of the people in the world are poor, and secretly resent the wealth of the other tenth.'
39. *His Prehistoric Past* (see film index).
40. Sam Mintz, 'The "Gag", or Fire, Wire and Water', *Intercine*, 3 (March 1935), p. 144.
41. There is no article by Joseph Gregor in *Intercine*. However, cf. his *Weltgeschichte des Theaters* (Zürich: Phaidon, 1933), p. 39.
42. Bardèche and Brasillach, op. cit., p. 215.
43. Cf. Rotha, op. cit., pp. 66f. and 129ff.
44. 'Vorrede zu "Oaha" ' in *Werke*, Band 3, Prosa (Berlin: Aufbau-Verlag, 1969), p. 356.
45. 'Notes' in *The Threepenny Opera*, trans. Desmond I. Vesey and Eric Bentley (New York: Grove Press, 1964), p. 103.

46. Ferdinand Hardekopf, 'Gastspiel Frank Wedekind', *Pan*, Jg.1, Nr.20 (16 August, 1911), p. 673.
47. Arnheim, op. cit., pp. 211–14.
48. Bardèche and Brasillach, op. cit., p. 245.

Hans Richter filmography

Unless otherwise stated, direction, script and graphic design are in each case by Hans Richter.

1920   Untitled experimental film based on the scroll picture *Präludium*, made in the UFA animation studio; length c. 10 mins.

1921   *Rhythmus 21* (originally: *Film ist Rhythmus*); black and white; use of negative film as positive; length c. 4 mins.
First shown by van Doesburg in Paris in 1921.

1923   *Rhythmus 23*; black and white; photography by Charles Métain; length c. 5 mins.
First shown by Hans Richter in Paris (Théâtre Michel) in 1923.

1925   *Rhythmus 25*; black and white, hand-tinted; based on the scroll picture *Orchestration der Farbe* (1923); photography by Charles Métain; length c. 4 mins.

1925-6   *Filmstudie*; photography by Hans Richter and Endrejat, musical accompaniment composed by H. H. Stuckenschmidt, arranged by Ernst Toch (later, in a short version, set to Darius Milhaud's *La Création du monde*); length c. 7 mins.

1926   Contribution to an American woman film-maker's film *Hands*, not used in the final version of the film. Richter's first film commission. *Trademark* (leader) for the films of the sensational actor Albertini.

1926-9   Large numbers of advertising films, including some for the 'Epoche' agency (e.g. *Bauen und Wohnen*, photography by Otto Tober), for the building contractor Sommerfeld, for Muratti cigarettes. 'I tried to develop some new cinematographic element in each of these films' (Hans Richter).

1927   Kasimir Malevich provides an outline for a film with Richter: *Die Malerei und die Probleme der Architektur*; a realisation, photography by Arnold Keagle, begun in the USA in 1970, not completed.

1927-8   *Inflation* (introductory film for the fiction film *Die Dame mit der Maske*, directed by Wilhelm Thiele); production company UFA; photography by Charles Métain; black and white; silent; original length c. 20 mins., reduced to 8 mins.
Richter's first essay film.
Vormittagsspuk (Ghosts before Noon, *usually translated as* Ghosts before Breakfast); production company (later as a sound film) Tobis; photography by Reimar Kuntze; music by Paul Hindemith (performed by the orchestra with the help of a synchronised unrolling score constructed by the Swiss composer Robert Blum); actors Paul

169

Hindemith, Werner Graeff, Richter, Darius and Madelaine Milhaud, Jean Oser, Walter Gronostay; original outline by Werner Graeff; black and white; length: about 10 mins.

Made for the Baden-Baden International Music Festival.

1928–9 *Rennsymphonie* (introductory film for the fiction film *Ariadne im Hoppegarten*, directed by Robert Dinesen); production company Maxim-Emelka; photography by Max Tober; original length 18 mins., reduced to 7 mins.

1928–9 *Zweigroschenzauber*; advertising film for the *Kölnische Illustrierte Zeitung*; black and white; silent; length c. 8 mins.

1929 *Alles dreht sich, alles bewegt sich*; documentary film; production company Tobis; script by Richter and Werner Graeff; photography by Reimar Kuntze; music by Walter Gronostay; black and white; sound; length c. 28 mins.

The Storming of La Sarraz; shot together with S. M. Eisenstein, Edvard Tisse, Aleksandrov and others during the Congress of Independent Cinema in La Sarraz; not finished and subsequently lost (if there was any film in the cameras?).

Everyday (completed 1968 and 1975); shot with the participation of a 'Workshop' in London; actors S. M. Eisenstein, Len Lye et al.; black and white; sound; length c. 30 mins.

1920–30 *Neues Leben*; documentary film for the Swiss Werkbund in Zurich; photography by Emil Berna; silent; two reels.

1931 *Europa Radio*; documentary film for the Dutch firm Philips in Eindhoven; photography by Charles Métain; music by Walter Gronostay; length two reels.

Distributed in about 40 different (sound) versions at the time.

1931–3 *Metall*; semi-documentary fiction film about the strike at Hennings-dorf (near Berlin), made with the assistance of some of the strikers; German-Russian co-production, production companies Prometheus and Mezhrabpomfilm; script by Richter and Pera Attasheva; photography by Ketelnikov; sound; planned length c. ten reels; unfinished.

1933 *Hallo Everybody*; documentary film for Philips; assistant director John Fernhout (or Ferno); photography by Alexander von Barsy; music by Darius Milhaud (performed by the Philips Orchestra under Robert Blum); length c. three reels.

1933–4 *Keine Zeit für Tränen*; project (Paris) with the actress Margarete Melzer in mind; script by Anna Seghers, Friedrich Kohner and Richter.

1934 *Candide*; project (Paris), based on Voltaire's satire.

1936 *Vom Blitz zum Fernsehbild*; documentary film for Philips; photography by Alexander von Barsy; music by Darius Milhaud; length c. two reels.

1937   *Baron Münchhausen*; project (Zurich); sets by Georges Méliès.

1938   *Hans im Glück*; production company Central-Film; actors Emil Hegetschwiler, Alfred Rasser.

1939   *Die Lügen des Baron Münchhausen*; project (Basel); production company Frobenius; script by Richter, Jacques Prévert, Jacques Brunius, Maurice Henry; actors Michel Simon, Pierre Brasseur, Jules Berry.

Die Börse als Markt (*Die Börse*); production company Frobenius; technical collaborator Heinrich Burckhardt; opening music by Wolfgang Laroche.

1939–41   Many further advertising films for Central-Film in Zurich.

1941   *The Monroe Doctrine*; project (New York); script by Richter and Kenneth White.

The Four Freedoms; project (New York); on the 'four freedoms' of Roosevelt's speech.

The Role of Women in America; project (New York).

1944   *The Movies Take a Holiday*; anthology of the cinematic avant-garde assembled by Richter and Herman G. Weinberg from films by René Clair, Jean Renoir, Marcel Duchamp, Fernand Léger, Man Ray, Richter and others; length c. 65 mins.; unfinished.

1945   *The Story of the Unicorn*; project (New York); about the unicorn as a mystical animal symbol of love in the nineteenth century; production company Metropolitan Museum of Modern Art; co-worker Suzanne Hare.

1945–6   *The Accident*; project (New York); test film on the theme of race discrimination; script by Richter and Siegfried Kracauer for the American Jewish Committee.

1946–7   Filming of Kurt Schwitter's *Ursonate*; unfinished, later incorporated as a fragment in *Dadascope*.

1944–7   *Dreams that Money Can Buy*; episode film in colour; production company Art of this Century Corp. (=Peggy Guggenheim, Kenneth Macpherson, Richter); outlines of the individual episodes:

1. *Desire:* Max Ernst
2. *The Girl with the Prefabricated Heart:* Fernand Léger
3. *Ruth, Roses and Revolvers:* Man Ray
4. *Color Records and Nudes Descending a Staircase:* Marcel Duchamp
5. *A Ballet in the Universe:* Alexander Calder
6. *Circus:* Alexander Calder
7. *Narcissus:* Hans Richter

Photography by Arnold Eagle (Kodachrome in 1, 2, 4, 5, 7), Meyer Rosenblum (3), Herman Shulman (3), Peter Gluchanok (6), Werner Brandes, Victor Vicas; music by Paul Bowles (1, 5), Libby Holman and Josh White (2), Darius Milhaud (3), John Cage (4), Edgar Varèse

(5), David Diamond (6), Lou Applebaum (7), Duke Ellington; actors Max Ernst (1), Joe Maison (1), Julian Levy (1), Arthur Seymour (3), Ruth Sobotka (3), Bill Frankel (3), Evelyn Hausman (3), Alexander Calder (6), Jack Bittner (7), Dorothy Griffith (7), Jacqueline Matisse; length 88 mins.; 1947 Venice Biennale Prize for the best contribution to the progress of cinematography.

1948   *The Minotaur*; project (New York); for a film version of the Greek myth of the minotaur.

1951–61   *Forty* (originally *Thirty*) *Years of Experiment*; in two parts; Part I: Anthology of ten experimental films and film fragments by Richter dating from the years 1921–31, excerpts from Eggeling's *Diagonal-Symphonie* (short version) and (?) Ruttmann's *Opus 4*; length 32 mins.; Part II: Excerpts from *Dreams that Money Can Buy* and the shooting of it (*Six Modern Artists Make a Film*), *8×8* and *Dadascope*; colour; length 30 mins.

1956–7   *8×8*; photography by Arnold Eagle; music by Robert Abrahamson, John Gruen, Richter, Douglas Townsend; actors Jean Cocteau, Paul Bowles, Jacqueline Matisse, Alexander Calder, Hans Arp, Yves Tanguy, Julian Levy, Richard Huelsenbeck, Max Ernst, José L. Sert, Frederick Kiesler; colour; length 88 mins.
Chesscetera (*Passionate Passtime*); speaker Vincent Price; actors Darius Milhaud, Marcel Duchamp, Larry Evans; length 28 mins.

1956   *Dadascope* (Parts I and II); film collage to dada poems; with original sound recordings of Arp, Duchamp, Raoul Haussmann, Huelsenbeck, Schwitters, Man Ray, Richter, Georges Ribemont-Dessaignes, Marcel Janco, Walter Mehring and Theo van Doesburg; actors Duchamp, Arp, Huelsenbeck, Tanguy; length 52 mins.

1962   *Alexander Calder: from the Circus to the Moon*; combination of Calder's contributions to the films *Dreams that Money Can Buy* and *8×8*.

Assembled from information given by Hans Richter and by the filmographies in Hans Richter: *Filmgegner von heute – Filmfreunde von morgen*, Reprint, Zürich, 1968, pp. 132ff., and Hans Scheugl and Ernst Schmidt jr., *Eine Subgeschichte des Films* (Frankfurt-am-Main: 1974), Band 2, pp. 739ff.
Almost all the films made before 1941 either survive only in fragments or have been completely lost.

The following films by Hans Richter are distributed in Britain:
Dreams that Money Can Buy. Connoisseur Films, c/o Harris Films, Surrey.
Forty Years of Experiment. German Film Library, c/o Viscom, London.
Ghosts before Breakfast. British Film Institute.
Rhythm 21. British Film Institute.

Rhythm 21, *Rhythm 23* and *Film Study* are available on the compilation reels 'German Abstract Animation', with films by Walther Ruttmann. Concord, Ipswich; further details may be obtained from the Arts Council Film Office, London.

Hans Richter bibliography

This bibliography lists all the books, contributions to journals and manuscripts *by* Hans Richter known to the editor; and also interviews. It is arranged chronologically according to the date of first publication or, in the case of unpublished manuscripts, according to the date of writing. Translations always immediately follow the date of first publication.

Books

1. *Universelle Sprache.* Pamphlet. Written in collaboration with Viking Eggeling. Forst in der Lausitz, 1920. (About 8 pages.)
2. *Filmgegner von heute – Filmfreunde von morgen.* Berlin, 1929. Reprint: Zurich, 1968 (with bio-filmography and bibliography). Programmatic text for the film section of the Stuttgart Werkbund exhibition of 18 May to 17 July 1929.
3. *Film: jesteren, heden, morgen.* Pamphlet for the Dutch Filmliga. Special number of the magazine *Filmliga.* Amsterdam, 1935.
4. *Der Kampf um den Film.* Written in Carabietta, Switzerland, 1934–9. First published Munich 1976.
5. *Film and Progress.* American version of *Der Kampf um den Film.* Prepared in collaboration with Herman G. Weinberg; unfinished; about 1942.
6. *The Struggle for the Film.* English translation of *Der Kampf um den Film.* London and New York 1986.
7. *Dada-Profile.* Zurich, 1961 (Sammlung Horizont).
8. *Dada, Kunst und Antikunst.* Cologne, 1964. Third, revised and expanded edition, 1973.
9. *Dada, Art and Anti-Art.* Translated by David Britt. London, 1965. One of many translations into various languages of *Dada, Kunst und Antikunst.*
10. *Dada 1916–1966. Dokumente der internationalen Dada-Bewegung.* Catalogue of the Goethe Institute exhibition. Compiled and annotated by Hans Richter. Cologne/Munich, 1966.
11. *Köpfe und Hinterköpfe.* Zurich, 1967.
12. *Hans Richter by Hans Richter.* Edited by Cleve Gray. Illustrated volume of memoirs and reminiscences by Richter about his life and work. New York, 1971.
13. *Begegnungen von Dada bis heute. Briefe, Dokumente, Erinnerungen.* Cologne, 1973.

Articles

14. *Vorwort* to the XXIX. Kollektiv-Ausstellung. Hans Richter, Strohmeyer, Lascar Vorel. Munich: Galerie Neue Kunst Hans Goltz, 7 June to 8 July 1916, pp. 3–4.

15. *Ein Maler spricht zu den Malern.* Zeitecho (Bern), Vol. 3 (1917), 1 and 2 June Numbers, pp. 19–23.

16. *Gegen Ohne Für Dada.* Dada (Zurich), n. 4–5, February 1919, p. 22. Reprint: Rome/Milan, 1970.

1920

17. *Prinzipielles zur Bewegungskunst.* De Stijl (Leiden), Vol. 4 (1921), n. 7, pp. 109–12. Also in De Stijl Reprint: Amsterdam/The Hague, 1968, Band 1, pp. 81–9; and Hans L. C. Jaffé: Mondrian und De Stijl. Cologne, 1967, pp. 135–7.

18. *Erklärung vor dem Kongress der Internationale Fortschrittlicher Künstler Düsseldorf* for 30 May 1922. Signed by Hans Richter. De Stijl (Leiden), Vol. 5 (1922), n. 4 (Reprint), pp. 203–4.

19. *Film.* De Stijl (Leiden), Vol. 5 (1922), n. 6, pp. 91f. Reprint: p. 228. Jaffé: pp. 171–3.

20. *K. I. Konstruktivistische Internationale schöpferische Arbeitsgemeinschaft.* Dated: Weimar, September 1922. Signed by Theo van Doesburg, Richter, El Lissitzky, Karel Maes, Max Burchartz. (With translations into French and Dutch.) De Stijl (Leiden), Vol. 5 (1922), no. 8, pp. 113–19. Reprint: pp. 247–50.

21. *Film.* De Stijl (Leiden), Vol. 6 (1923), n. 5, pp. 55f. Reprint: p. 377. Jaffé: pp. 188f.

22. *Constructivism* (Magyar), MA (Vienna), Vol. 8 (1923), n. 9–10, p. [4f.].

23. *G. Zeitschrift für elementaren Gestaltung.* Edited by Hans Richter. Berlin, 1923–6, five numbers in all (nn. 1–5/6).

The following articles by Hans Richter appeared in *G.*:

23.1 *Material zur elementaren Gestaltung.* N.1, pp. 1f.; n. 3, pp. 1ff.

23.2 *Die Eroberung der Maschinen.* N. 3, p. 24.

23.3 *Prag.* N. 3, p. 28.

23.4 *Die schlecht trainierte Seele.* N. 3, pp. 34–7. Also in Richard Huelsenbeck: Dada – Eine literarische Dokumentation. Reinbek, 1964, pp. 96–100. English translation: Image (Cambridge), October 1965, pp. 18f.

23.5 *Kurt Schwitters.* N. 3, p. 47.

23.6 *Arp.* N. 3, p. 49.

23.7 *'De Stijl'.* N. 3, p. 58.

23.8 *L'Esprit Nouveau.* N. 3, p. 60.

23.9 *Der Querschnitt.* N. 3, p. 61.

23.10 *An den Konstruktivismus.* N. 3, p. 62.

23.11 *(Vorwort).* N. 4, p. 1.

23.12 *Arp und die elementare Gestaltung.* N. 4, p. 9.

23.13   *Die Kunst von heute: Ausstellung abstrakter Kunst, Paris, Dezember 1925*. N. 4, pp. 11–14.

23.14   *Viking Eggeling*. N. 4, pp. 14ff.

23.15   (Film manifesto, signed 'G'). N. 5, pp. 1f.

23.16   (Notes). N. 5, p. 6.

23.17   *Dimension*. N. 5, p. 8.

23.18   *Teil einer Partitur zu dem Film Rhythmus 25*. N. 5, p. 11.

23.19   *Fuge aus einem absoluten Film (I)*. N. 5, p. 17.

23.20   *Die eigentliche Sphäre des Films*. N. 5, p. 18.

23.21   *Kitsch ist nahrhaft*. N. 5, p. 20.

23.22   *Bisher*. N. 5, p. 23.

23.23   *Geschichte ist das, was heute geschieht*. N. 5, p. 24.

23.24   *Die reine Form ist die Natürliche*. N. 5, pp. 27f.

23.25   *Die Nutte siegt*. N. 5, p. 31.

23.1.1 An author index to the five numbers of G has appeared as *Great Little Magazines, No. 3: 'G'* in Form (Cambridge), n. 3, December 1966, pp. 26ff.

23.1.2 Literature on the 'G Group': Werner Graeff: *Concerning the so-called G Group*. Art Journal (New York), Vol. 23 (1964), n. 4, pp. 280ff. A reply to the above: Raoul Haussmann: *More on Group 'G'*. College Art Journal (New York), Vol. 24 (1965), n. 4, pp. 350ff. A German version of the Graeff article has appeared in *Werk und Zeit* (Krefeld) (no further details available).

24.   *Rhythm*. Little Review (New York). Winter 1926, p. 21.

25.   According to n. 11, p. 173, Hans Richter was art, music and film editor for the Berlin daily paper *Tägliche Rundschau*. From 28 December 1926 to 1 April 1928, a Johannes M. Richter edited the weekly page entitled 'Kino und Kultur'. Nearly all the contributions to this page are signed 'R.', 'H.R.' or 'R . . . r'.

When asked the explanation for this differentiation, and whether Johannes M. Richter is identical with Hans Richter, the latter could no longer remember.

26.   *Neue Mittel der Filmgestaltung*. Die Form (Berlin), Vol. 4 (1929), n. 3, pp. 53–6. Also in Felix Schwarz. Frank Gloor, ed.: 'Die Form'. Gütersloh, 1969, pp. 230ff.

27.   *Aufgaben eines Filmstudios*. Die Form (Berlin), Vol. 4 (1929), p. 72.

28.   *Der absolute Film braucht die Industrie*. An interview with Hans Richter. Film-Kurier (Berlin), Vol. 10, n. 6, 5 January 1929.

29.   *Avantegarde im Bereich des Möglichen*. Film-Kurier (Berlin), special number 'Zehn Jahre Film-Kurier', 1 June 1929.

30.   *Film von Morgen*. Das Werk (Zurich), Vol. 16 (1929), n. 9, pp. 278–84. Polish translation as *Film Jutra*. Praesens (Warsaw), n. 2, May 1930, pp. 160–65.

1930

31. *Richtigstellung*. Lichtbildbühne (Berlin), 2 April 1930. (Reply to a review of one of his lectures in Film-Kurier, 8 March 1930.)

32. *L'Objet et lemouvement*. Cercle et Carré (Paris), 15 March 1930. Also in Michel Seuphor, ed.: Cercle et Carré. Paris, 1971, pp. 133ff.

33. *Reader's letter* about the shooting of 'Romance Sentimentale'. Film-Kurier (Berlin), Vol. 12, n. 212, 8 September 1930.

34. *Der Film – eine Ware*. Arbeiterbühne und Film (Berlin), 1931, n. 4, pp. 24ff. Reprint: Cologne, 1974.

35. *Von der statischen zur dynamischen Form*. Plastique (Paris), 1937, n. 2, pp. 12–18. Also in Huelsenbeck (cf. n. 23.4), pp. 250ff.

36. *Kulturfilm als Kunst*. Der Geistesarbeiter (Zürich), Vol. 17, April 1938, pp. 49–55.

37. *La Vie courte mais féconde du film d'avantgarde*. Unpublished manuscript, dated July 1939, 6 pp.

1940

38. *Wahrheit im Film*. Neue Zürcher Zeitung (Zurich), n. 60, 14 January 1940, sheet 3.

39. *Urkino*. Neue Zürcher Zeitung (Zurich), n. 281, 25 February 1940, sheet 6.

40. *Ur-Kino II*. Neue Zürcher Zeitung (Zurich), n. 599, 21 April 1940, sheet 6.
    Nn. 38, 39 and 40 consist in part of advance publications from *Der Kampf um den Film*.

41. *Der Film Essay: Eine neue Form des Dokumentarfilms*. Nationalzeitung (Basel), 25 April 1940, supplement.

42. *Quelques instants avec Hans Richter avant son départ pour l'Amérique*. Interview with Serge Lang. La Revue de l'Écran (Paris), Vol. 4, n. 387-B, 3 April 1941, p. 5.

43. *Post-War Planning and Documentary Film*. Unpublished manuscript of c. 1941, 11pp.

44. *Der politische Film*. Deutsche Blätter (Santiago de Chile), Vol. 2 (1944), n. 1, pp. 21–4 and n. 2, pp. 17–20. Also in Karsten Witte, ed.: Theorie des Kinos. Frankfurt-am-Main, 1972, pp. 61–78.

45. *From Orchestration of the Form to Scroll Painting*. Exhibition catalogue 'Masters of Abstract Art'. Helena Rubinstein Benefit for the Red Cross, New York City, March 1943.

46. *Cinéma américain d'Avant-garde*. Style en France (Paris). Special number 'Cinéma', n. 4, July–August–September 1946, pp. 96f.

47. *Voir du merveilleux*. La Revue du Cinéma (Paris), Vol. 2 (1947), n. 7, pp. 15–18. Also in Pierre Lherminier: L'Art du cinéma. Paris, 1960, p. 468.

48. *A History of the Avantgarde*. Frank Stauffacher, ed.: Art in Cinema. San Francisco, 1947 (Reprint: New York, 1970), pp. 6–21.

177

49. *Avantgarde Film in Germany.* Roger Manvell, ed.: Experiment in the Film. London, 1948 (Reprint: New York, 1970), pp. 218–33.
German version: *Der avantgardistische Film in Deutschland (von 1921–1951).* Cineaste (Göttingen), special number Deutsche Filmtage Göttingen 1953, pp. 13–23.

50. *The Avantgarde Film Seen from Within.* Hollywood Quarterly (Berkeley), Vol. 4, n. 1, Fall 1949, pp. 34–41.

1950

51. *Minnesord.* (On V. Eggeling). Catalogue for the exhibition 'Viking Eggeling 1880 bis 1925. Technare och filmkonstuar'. Stockholm, 27 October to 19 November 1950, pp. 9f.

52. *Dada XYZ.* Robert Motherwell, ed.: The Dada Painters and Poets. New York, 1951, pp. 283–90. (Written in 1948.)

53. *The Film as an Original Art Form.* College Art Journal (New York), Vol. 10 (1951), n. 2, pp. 157–61.
German version: *Der Film als selbständige Kunstform.* Exhibition Catalogue, Bibliography n. 102, pp. 3–9. Also in Gottfried Schlemmer, ed.: Avantgardistischer Film 1951–1971. Munich, 1973, pp. 16ff.
French version: *Un Art original. Le Film.* Cahiers du Cinéma (Paris), Vol. 2, n. 10, March 1952, pp. 11–15.
Italian version: *Il film arte originale.* Sette Arte (Ivrea), Vol. 1 (1952), n. 1, pp. 73f.

54. *Il film come forma d'arte originale.* La Biennale di Venezia (Venice), n. 4, April 1951, pp. 29f.

55. *Anatomie de l'avant-garde.* L'Age du Cinéma (Paris), n. 3, June–July 1951, pp. 3–6.

56. *Histoire de l'avant-garde allemand.* L'Age du Cinéma (Paris), n. 6, 1951, pp. 20–24. (Revised version of n. 49.)

57. *Vita privata del movimento 'dada' 1916–1918.* La Biennale di Venezia (Venice), January 1952, n. 7, pp. 16–21.

58. *Easel – Scroll – Film.* Magazine of Art (Washington), Vol. 45 (1952), February, pp. 78–86. (Original manuscript 8 pp.)

59. *Funzione del cinema sperimentale.* Cinema (Milan), n. 97, 1 November 1952, pp. 222–6.

60. *Il film di avanguardia il film astratto e il futurismo.* Cinema Italiano (Rome), n. 12, December 1953, pp. 39–44. (Original manuscript *The Avantegardefilm and Futurism* dated July 1953, 5pp.) Reply to an article by Bragaglia in Cinema Italiano n. 3 (1953).

61. *Max Ernst: sincerità – serietà – immaginazione – gioia.* La Biennale di Venezia (Venice), nn. 19–20, April 1954, pp. 32–6.

62. *Otto storie sugli scacchi.* La Biennale di Venezia (Venice), n. 22, September–October 1954, pp. 15–20.

63. *Film as an Original Art.* Film Culture (New York), n. 1, January 1955,

pp. 19–23. Also in P. Adams Sitney, ed.: Film Culture Reader. New York, 1970, pp. 15–20. And in Richard Dyer MacCann, ed.: Film – A Montage of Theories. New York, 1966, pp. 180–86.

64. *Eight Free Improvisations on the Game of Chess.* Film Culture (New York), Vol. 1 (1955), n. 1, January 1955, pp. 36ff.

65. *Frank Stauffacher.* Film Culture (New York), Vol. 1, nn. 5–6, Winter 1955, pp. 4f.

66. *8 × 8. Hans Richter's Latest Experimental Film.* (Excerpt from the Script.) Film Culture (New York), Vol. 1, nn. 5–6, Winter 1955, pp. 17ff.

67. *Theory and Experiment in the Modern Film.* Otto Molden, ed.: Erkenntnis und Aktion. Vorträge und Gespräche des Europäischen Forum Alpbach 1955, Berlin, 1955, pp. 190–204.

68. *Fernand Léger 1881–1955.* College Art Journal (New York), Vol. 15 (1956), n. 4, pp. 340–43.

69. *Yves Tanguy.* College Art Journal (New York), Vol. 15 (1956), n. 4, pp. 343–6.
   Nn. 68 and 69 together entitled *In Memory of Two Friends.*

70. *Fernand Léger.* La Biennale di Venezia (Venice), n. 27, March 1956, pp. 5f.

71. *Yves Tanguy.* La Biennale di Venezia (Venice), n. 27, March 1956, pp. 27f. Nn. 70 and 71 probably identical with nn. 68 and 69.

72. *8 × 8. An Interview with Hans Richter by Gideon Bachmann.* Film and TV Music (New York), Vol. 16, n. 2, Winter 1956, pp. 19f.

73. *Beginnings of German Abstraction.* The American Abstract Artists, ed.: The World of Abstract Art. New York, 1957, pp. 37–40.

74. *30 Years of Film Poetry. Selfexpression and Communication.* Unpublished manuscript, c. 1957, 8pp.

75. *Hans Richter on the Nature of Film Poetry. An Interview with Jonas Mekas.* Film Culture (New York), Vol. 3, n. 1 (complete series, n. 11) (1957), pp. 5–8.

76. *8 × 8.* Cinema Nuovo (Milan), Vol. 4, n. 113, 1 September 1957, pp. 118f.

77. *Al posto del cannone la macchina da scrivere.* Cinema Nuovo (Milan), Vol. 4, nn. 114–15, 15 September 1957, pp. 164f.

78. *Film as a Part of Modern Art.* Essay by Hans Richter submitted for Graham Foundation Grant. New York, 1958. Unpublished, 2pp.

79. *Filmen son konstform.* K. G. Hultén, ed.: Apropá Eggeling. Stockholm, 1958, pp. 8–14.

80. *Om Viking Eggeling.* K. G. Hultén, ed.: Apropá Eggeling. Stockholm, 1958, pp. 15ff.

81. *8 × 8.* Catalogue for the exhibition 'Fifth Avenue Theatre'. New York, 1958. German version in n. 105.

82. *A Clowning Out of the Void.* (Review of the American edition of Willy

Verkauf's *Dada* volume.) Saturday Review (New York), 1 February 1958, p. 20.

83. *Glorified Juke Box and Activated Sound.* Herald Tribune (New York), March 1958. Manuscript, 4pp.

84. *On the Function of Film History Writing.* Film Culture (New York), Vol. 4, n. 3 (complete series, n. 18), April 1958, pp. 25f.

85. *Dada und Film.* Willy Verkauf, ed.: Dada. Monographie einer Bewegung. Teufen, Switzerland, 1958, ²1965, pp. 57–66.

86. *Der Zufall.* Karl Heinz Hering, Ewald Rathke, ed.: Dada. Dokumentation einer Bewegung (Exhibition catalogue), Düsseldorf, 1958, pp. [104f.].

87. *Dada ist tot, es lebe Dada.* Magnum (Cologne), n. 22 (1959), p. 11.

88. *Experiment als Lebenselexier. Ein Gespräch mit Hans Richter von Willy Rotzler.* Die Weltwoche (Zurich), Vol. 27 (1959), n. 1321, 6 March 1959, p. 5.

89. *Peinture et film.* XXᵉ Siècle (Paris), n. 12, May–June 1959, pp. 25–8.

90. *Gespräch mit Hans Richter von Friedrich Bayl.* Art International (Zurich), Vol. 3 (1959), nn. 1–2, pp. 54f.

1960

91. *Vorwort* to Adrien de Menasce Exhibition, Zürich: Galerie Charles Lienhard, 10 February to 12 March 1960, pp. 3f.

92. Contribution on the theme 'Natur von Scroll und Film'. Suzanne K. Langer, ed.: Reflections on Art. New York, 1961.

93. *Dichter, Denker, Dadaisten.* DU (Zurich), Vol. 21 (1961), April, pp. 55ff. (Advance publication from n. 7).

94. *Intervju med Hans Richter* by L. Sjöberg. Konstrevy (Stockholm), Vol. 37 (1961), n. 3, pp. 88–93.

95. *Je ne suis pas un cinéaste . . .* Positif (Paris), n. 40, July 1961, pp. 1ff.

96   *Be Be* (=Bewegte Bewegung). Blätter und Bilder (Würzburg), n. 13, March–May 1961, pp. 48–53.

97. *From Interviews with Hans Richter During the Last Ten Years* (by Jonas Mekas, Gideon Bachmann and the Danish Film Museum). Film Culture (New York), n. 31, Winter 1963–4, pp. 26–35.

98. *Dalla pittura moderna al cinema moderno.* La Biennale di Venezia (Venice), n. 54, September 1964, pp. 3–13.

99. *Introduzione a 'Dadascope'.* La Città (Venice), n. 3, June 1964, pp. 53f.

100. *Dadaismo – Surrealismo – Cinema Sperimentale.* La Città (Venice), n. 3, June 1964, pp. 59–68.

101. *My Experience with Movement in Painting and Film.* György Kepes, ed.: The Nature and Art of Motion. New York, 1965. Manuscript, 11pp.
German version: *Meine Erfahrungen mit Bewegung in Malerei und*

Film. György Kepes, ed.: Wesen und Kunst der Bewegung. Brussels, 1969, pp. 142–57.

102. *Témoignages: Hans Richter*. Études Cinématographiques, nn. 38–9: Le Film surréaliste. Paris, 1965, pp. 55f.

103. *Arp se levant derrière un nuage*. Catalogue for the exhibition 'Jean Arp – Hans Richter'. Paris: Galerie Denise René, 28 April 1965.

104. *Stolpern*. Neue Zürcher Zeitung (Zurich), nn. 494–5, morning edition of 5 February 1966, sheets 5f.

105. Catalogue for the exhibition 'Hans Richter – Maler und Filmschöpfer'. Berlin: Akademie der Künste/DDFB, 20–21 March 1967.

106 *Bemerkungen zu meinen Arbeiten*. Hamburger Filmgespräche, Vol. III. Hamburg, 1967, pp. 19–24.

107. *Begegnungen in Berlin*. Catalogue for the exhibition 'Avantgarde Osteuropa 1910/1930'. Berlin: Deutsche Gesellschaft für Bildende Kunst/Akademie der Künste, 1967, pp. 13–21.

108. *Step by Step*. Studies in the Twentieth Century (Troy, N.Y.), n. 2, Fall 1968, pp. 7–20. Also in Form (Cambridge), n. 9, April 1969, pp. 21–5.

109. *L'Avant-garde allemande des années vingt*. Bianco e Nero (Rome), nn. 9–10 (1968), pp. 227–32.

110. *In Memory of Marcel Duchamp*. Form (Cambridge), n. 9, April 1969, pp. 4f.

111. *Ich ueber mich*. Civiltà delle macchine (Rome), Vol. 17, n. 3, May–June 1969, pp. 37–48.

112. *In Memory of a Friend* (Marcel Duchamp). Art in America (New York), Vol. 57 (1969), n. 4, July–August 1969, pp. 40f.

1970

113. *The World Between the Ox and the Swine. Dada Drawings by Hans Richter*. Bulletin of Rhode Island School of Design (Providence, R.I.), Vol. 57, nn. 3 and 4, August 1971, 56pp.
(Exhibition catalogue with very detailed commentary by Hans Richter.)

114. *Pittura moderna: cinema moderno 1910–1970/Modern Painting: Modern Film 1910–1970. Dynamism and Kinetism*. Quintaparete (Turin), n. 3, January 1972, pp. 8ff., 12f. (bilingual).

The following items are occasionally listed in bibliographies, but could not be located in the sources referred to:

115. *Avantgarde: History and Dates of the Only Independent Artists Film Movement 1921–1931*. Unpublished manuscript.
In the possession of neither Hans Richter himself nor of the Hans Richter Archive in the Museum of Modern Art, New York.

116. *Der Ursprung des Avantgarde-Films*. F.A. (=Film Artystycvy) (Warsaw), n. 2, 1937.

Only two issues of this journal seem to have appeared Neither contains an article by Hans Richter.

117. *Origine de l'avant-garde allemand.* Cinématographe (Paris), May 1937. No trace of this could be found (according to Bibliothèque Nationale).

118. *From Painting to Film, from Film to Painting.* Magazine of Art (Washington), February 1952.

119. *Painting – Scroll – Film.* Magazine of Art (Washington), 1953. Nn. 118 and 119 are probably both identical to n. 58. However, they are not to be found in the sources named.

In addition, all the catalogues to Hans Richter exhibitions contain statements by the artist. These are often texts written especially for the purpose and available nowhere else. The difficulty of obtaining the sources has meant that it is impossible to list these items individually.

Index of films

183

Le Dernier Milliardaire (France)
  directed by René Clair, with Max Dearly, Renée Saint-Cyr, Marthe Mellot, 1934. – 122
Dinner at Eight (USA)
  directed by George Cukor, with Marie Dressler, John Barrymore, Wallace Beery, Jean Harlow, 1933. – 121

Emak Bakia (France)
  produced, directed and photographed by Man Ray, 1927. – 60
Entr'acte (France)
  directed by René Clair for the ballet 'Relâche' by Francis Picabia, music by Eric Satie, with Jean Borlin, Inge Fries, Picabia, Man Ray, Marcel Duchamp, Eric Satie, George Auric, 1923. – 60, 155
L'Étoile de mer (France)
  produced, directed and photographed by Man Ray, from the poem of the same title by Robert Desnos, with Youki Desnos and André de la Rivière, 1928. – 60
Exhibition of Rare Flowers (?) – 45

Filmstudie (Germany)
  See Hans Richter Filmography. – 60
Fire at the Charity Bazaar (?) – 42
Fools First (USA)
  directed by Marshall Neilan, with Richard Dix, Claire Windsor, Claude Gillingwater, Raymond Griffith, Leo White, 1922. – 132

G-Men (USA)
  directed by William Keighley, with James Cagney, Margaret Lindsay, Ann Dvorak, 1935. – 135
The General Line (Staroe i novoe/General'naja linija, USSR)
  directed and scripted by S. M. Eisenstein, photographed by Edvard Tisse, with Marfa Lapkina, M. Ivanin, V. Buzenkov, 1926–9. – 76
La Grande Illusion (France)
  directed by Jean Renoir, with Jean Gabin, Pierre Fresnay, Erich Von Stroheim, 1937. – 126, 135

Hallelujah (USA)
  directed by King Vidor, with Daniel L. Haynes, Nina Mae McKinney, William Fountaine, 1929. – 159
His Prehistoric Past (USA)
  production company Keystone Film Co., with Charlie Chaplin, Mack Swain, 1914. – 129

184

It Happened One Night (USA)
  directed by Frank Capra, with Clark Gable, Claudette Colbert, Walter Connolly, 1934. – 88, 129

Joyless Street (Die freudlose Gasse, Germany)
  directed by G. W. Pabst, with Asta Nielsen, Greta Garbo, Werner Krauss, 1925. – 124, 128

Das Käthchen von Heilbronn (Germany, ?)
  directed by Oskar Messter, with Henny Porten. – 65

Kameradschaft/La Tragédie de la mine (Germany/France)
  directed by G. W. Pabst, with Fritz Kampers, Alexander Granach, Ernst Busch, 1931. – 135

King Lear (USA?)
  probably *Shakespeare's Tragedy King Lear* (USA), directed by William V. Ranous (?), with Maurice Costello, Julian Arthur, Edith Storey, Mary Fuller, 1909. – 67

Komsomol (USSR)
  directed by Joris Ivens, 1932. – 154

The Last Laugh (Der letzte Mann, Germany)
  directed by F. W. Murnau, with Emil Jannings, Maly Delschaft, Mae Hiller, 1924–5. – 83, 93

M (Mörder unter uns) (Germany)
  directed by Fritz Lang, with Peter Lorre, Ellen Widmann, Inge Landgut, Gustaf Gründgens, 1931. – 72

Man of Aran (Great Britain)
  directed, scripted and photographed by Robert and Frances Flaherty, 1932–4. – 48, 120, 143

March of Time (USA)
  newsreel series produced by Louis de Rochemont, 1934–43. – 51

Marie (Hungary/Germany)
  directed by Paul Fejös, with Annabella, 1932. – 141

Moana (A Romance of the Golden Age) (USA)
  directed, scripted and photographed by Robert and Frances Flaherty, 1923–6. – 48, 120

Modern Times (USA)
  directed and scripted by Charlie Chaplin, with Charlie Chaplin, Paulette Goddard, Henry Bergman, 1936. – 128, 130, 140

Mister Deeds Goes to Town (USA)
  directed by Frank Capra, with Gary Cooper, Jean Arthur, George Bancroft, 1936. – 99–100, 128, 135, 137

The Mother (Mat', USSR)
 directed by Vsevolod Pudovkin, with Vera Baranovskaja, Nikolaj Balatov, A. Chistjakov, 1926. – 162
Music Land (USA)
 Walt Disney cartoon in the series *Silly Symphonies*, 1935. – 59

Nanook of the North (USA)
 directed, photographed and edited by Robert Flaherty, 1920–21. – 120, 143
Niemandsland (War is Hell, Germany)
 directed and scripted by Viktor Trivas, music by Hanns Eisler, Kurt Schröder, with Ernst Busch, Vladimir Sokoloff, Renée Stobrawa, 1931. The film was banned in 1933. – 162
No Greater Glory (USA)
 directed by Frank Borzage, with George Breakston, Jimmy Butler, Jackie Searl, 1934. – 107

La Passion de Jeanne d'Arc (The Passion of Joan of Arc, France)
 directed by Carl Theodor Dreyer, with Falconetti, Eugène Silvain, Maurice Schutz, 1926–8. – 116
The Private Life of Henry VIII (Great Britain)
 directed by Alexander Korda, with Charles Laughton, Robert Donat, Lady Tree, 1933. – 150–1, 155

Rhythmus 21 (Germany)
 see Hans Richter filmography. – 152
The River (USA)
 directed by Pare Lorentz, 1937. – 51
Le Roman d'un tricheur (France)
 directed and scripted by Sacha Guitry, with Sacha Guitry, Jacqueline Delubac, Pierre Assy, 1936. – 122, 139, 149

Secrets of a Soul (Geheimnisse einer Seele, ein psychoanalytischer Film, Germany)
 directed by G. W. Pabst, with Werner Krauss, Ruth Weyher, Ilka Grüning, 1925–6. – 56, 116
Skandal um Eva (Germany)
 directed by G. W. Pabst, with Henny Porten, Oskar Sima, Ludwig Stoessel, Paul Henckels, Adele Sandrock, 1930. – 42 n
The Student Prince (*In Old Heidelberg*) (USA)
 directed by Ernst Lubitsch, with Ramon Novarro, Norma Shearer, 1927. – 79, 95, 100, 113

Tartuffe (Tartüff, Germany)
 directed by F. W. Murnau, with Emil Jannings, Lil Dagover, Werner Krauss, Lucie Höflich, 1925–6. – 147

Thérèse Raquin/Du sollst nicht töten (Germany/France)
> directed by Jacques Feyder, with Gina Manès, Jeanne Marie-Laurent, Wolfgang Zilzer, 1927–8. – 83

Trouble in Paradise (USA)
> directed by Ernst Lubitsch, with Miriam Hopkins, Kay Francis, Herbert Marshall, Charles Ruggles, 1932. – 122

The Tsar's Arrival in Paris (France?)
> possibly *Les souvérains russes et le président de la République aux Champs-Élysées* or another subject from the section 'Fêtes Franco-Russes' in the 1896 catalogue of the Lumière Brothers; a fragment of a film on this subject is included in *Le Roman d'un tricheur*, q.v. – 42

Unter den Linden (France?)
> probably *Sous les tilleuls* (France), photographed by Eugène Promio (?) for the Lumière Brothers, 1896 or 1897. – 42

Variety (Variété, Germany)
> directed by E. A. Dupont, with Emil Jannings, Maly Delschaft, Lya de Putti, 1925. – 83

Viva Villa! (USA)
> directed by Jack Conway (and Howard Hawks), with Wallace Beery, Leo Carillo, Fay Wray, 1934. – 125, 135

Vormittagsspuk (Ghosts before Breakfast, Germany)
> see Hans Richter filmography. – 60

War in China (?) – 45

The Wedding March (USA)
> directed, scripted and edited by Erich Von Stroheim, with Erich Von Stroheim, Fay Wray, George Fawcett, 1926–8. – 124

The Whole Town's Talking (USA)
> directed by John Ford, with Edward G. Robinson, Jean Arthur, Wallace Ford, 1935. – 135

Work (USA)
> production company Essanay, with Charlie Chaplin and Charles Insley, 1915. – 60 n

Index of names

Arnheim, Rudolf (b. 1904), German–American film theoretician and psychologist of perception, has lived in the USA since 1939. – 37, 54, 79, 96, 109

Balázs, Béla (1884–1949), Hungarian theoretician of film and theatre, poet and scriptwriter, moved to Vienna in 1919, to Berlin in 1926, to Moscow in 1933, returning to Hungary in 1945. – 71

Brecht, Bertolt (1898–1956), German poet, playwright, theatre director and film scriptwriter, frequent contact with Richter in the 1920s. – 47, 105, 139

Canudo, Ricciotto (1877–1923), Italian writer, critic and film theoretician, lived in Paris from about 1905. – 119

Capra, Frank (b. 1897), American director, famous for his comedies. – 88, 135

Cavalcanti, Alberto (1897–1982), Brazilian director, in France in the 1920s, in the 1930s in Britain, returned to Brazil in 1949. – 52

Chaplin, Charles Spencer (1899–1977), English actor, director, writer and producer, moved to Hollywood in 1913, returned to England in 1952. – 60–62, 126–31, 140, 154–5

Clair, René (1898–1981), French director, a member of the avant-garde in the 1920s. – 59, 122–4, 135, 155, 159, 161

Colbert, Claudette (b. 1905), French actress, film star in Hollywood in the 1930s. – 89

Consiglio, Alberto. – 43 n

Cooper, Gary (1901–61), American actor, in films from 1925, sound film star. – 93

Coward, Noel (1899–1973), English actor, playwright, scriptwriter and director. – 120

Delacroix, Eugène (1798–1863), French painter and graphic artist. – 54

Delluc, Louis (1890–1924), French director, author and critic, close to the cinematic avant-garde. – 59

DeMille, Cecil Blount (1881–1959), American producer and director. – 70, 87

De Rochemont, Louis (1899–1978), American producer, founder and director (1934–43) of the documentary series *March of Time*. – 51 n

Dietrich, Marlene (b. 1902), German actress, in films from 1922, in Hollywood from 1930. – 93

Disney, Walt (1901–66), director, writer and producer of cartoon films, 'inventor' of Mickey Mouse and Donald Duck, film-maker from 1923. – 54, 59, 153

Dreyer, Carl Theodor (1889–1968), Danish film director, scriptwriter from 1912, directed his own films from 1920. – 116–17

Dulac, Germaine (1882–1942), French film directress, also known as a theoretician. – 116–17

Dupont, Ewald André (1891–1956), German director, originally a writer and critic, directed his own films from 1918, moved to the USA in 1929–30. – 83

Edison, Thomas Alva (1847–1931), American inventor, worked on his own system for photographing and projecting moving pictures from 1888, patented the Kinetoscope in 1891 and the Vitascope in 1896. – 63

Eggeling, Viking (1880–1925), Swedish draughtsman and painter, collaborated with Richter after 1918, among other things in experimental films. – 52

Ehrenburg, Ilja (1891–1967), Russian writer, moved to Paris in 1908, returned to the USSR about 1930. – 90

Eisenstein, Sergej Mikhailovich (1898–1948), Russian Theatre and film director, also theoretician, directed films from 1923. – 76, 135, 138–9, 162

Epstein, Jean (1897–1953), French director and theoretician, directed films from 1922. – 60

Fejös, Paul (1898–1963), Hungarian film director, mostly in the USA after 1923, no further films after 1945. – 141

Feyder, Jacques (1888–1948), French film director and scriptwriter, often worked abroad, originally an actor, directed his own films from 1916. – 83

Flaherty, Robert (1884–1951), American documentary film-maker, films from 1920. – 48–9, 120–1, 143

Gable, Clark (1901–60), American film actor from 1925, star from the 1930s. – 88–9, 93

Garbo, Greta (b. 1905), Swedish actress, worked in Sweden, Germany and, from 1925–41, in Hollywood, since 1941 she has lived in seclusion. – 93

Gaul, August (1869–1921) most famous sculptor of animals in Germany in his times. – 35

Gregor, Joseph (1888–1960), Austrian historian of theatre and cinema. – 136

Griffith, David Wark (1875–1948), American film director, originally actor, directed his own films from about 1908. – 69–70, 74, 75

Griffith, Raymond (1890–1957), American actor, director, producer and author, began in the Vitagraph film company in 1914. – 132

Guitry, Sacha (1885–1957), French theatre and film director, films from 1917, famous for his comedies. – 139, 149–50, 159

Hardekopf, Ferdinand (1876–1954), writer and translator, member of the *Die Aktion* group, a friend of Richter's from about 1913. – 149

Hardy, Oliver (1892–1957), American film comedian, mostly jointly with Stan Laurel. – 131

Hays, Will (1879–1954), head of the Motion Picture Producers Association of America, and especially of its censorship office from 1922–45. – 100

Histoire du Cinéma – 74, 85, 87, 140

Houdin, Robert. – 54

Intercine – 42, 132, 136

Ivens, Joris (b. 1898), Dutch documentarist, director of films from 1928. – 52, 144, 154

Jannings, Emil (1884–1950), German actor, parts in films from 1914, with Lubitsch in the USA from 1926–9. – 93, 147

Kaufman, Boris (1906–80), Russian cameraman, brother of Dziga Vertov, moved to France in 1928, to the USA in 1942. – 52

Keaton, Buster (1895–1966), American film comedian, also writer and director of his films. – 60

Keighley, William (1889–1984), American film director, originally theatre director, directing films from 1930. – 135

Lang, Fritz (1890–1976), German–American film director, in Hollywood from 1936. – 72

Laughton, Charles (1899–1962), English actor and director, in films from 1928, mostly in Hollywood since the 1930s. – 150–1, 155

Laurel, Stan (1890–1965), English actor, in films in Hollywood from 1918, mostly jointly with Oliver Hardy. – 131

Léger, Fernand (1881–1955), French painter and avant-garde film-maker, friend of Richter's. – 59

Linder, Max (1883–1925), French film comedian, scriptwriter and film director before 1914, cited by Chaplin as his model. – 82

Lorentz, Pare (1905–72), American documentary film-maker. – 51 n

Lubitsch, Ernst (1892–1947), German film director, originally a comic actor, directing films from 1913, in Hollywood from 1922–3, became a leading Paramount producer in the 1930s. – 121̂–2

Lumière, Louis (1894–1948) and Auguste (1862–1954), photographic equipment manufacturers, patented the Cinématographe in 1895, initiated the manufacture of films for their equipment. – 41–2, 63

Marx Brothers, team of film comedians of the American sound film in the 1930s and 1940s, including Leonard 'Chico' Marx (1891–1961), Arthur 'Harpo' Marx (1893–1964) and Julius 'Groucho' Marx (1895–1977). – 131

Meisel, Edmund (1874–1930), German composer and conductor. – 158